"Pat's message removes whatever excuse one might use as to why they can't succeed. I can't see why anyone serious about making it in the real estate business would not read this book."

—Floyd Wickman, National Speakers Hall of Fame;
over one million real estate audio programs sold

"Being a real estate coach I see good agents and great ones. Pat Hiban offers a step-by-step approach to take your business to the next benchmark. His game plan will help you build your business to 50 . . . 100 . . . 500 transactions."

—Dianna Kokoszka, president, MAPS Coaching

"Anyone who has sold over five hundred homes per year should be paid attention to by both the novice and highly experienced real estate agents."

—Craig Proctor, founder, Quantum Leap System

"This book applies to all types of small businesses. I have made it a must-read for all of our coaches and clients! Thanks for sharing your pain, successes, and family values!"

—Bob Corcoran, Corcoran Consulting and Coaching

"I have paid thousands of dollars to attend conferences where I have received less than 1 percent of the ideas that Pat Hiban's book provided me! A must-read!

—Ben Kinney, author of *Social* with Jay Papasan,
Social Media Futurist and top real estate agent

6 STEPS to 7 FIGURES

A Real Estate Professional's Guide
to Building Wealth *and*
Creating Your Own Destiny

PAT HIBAN

GREENLEAF
BOOK GROUP LLC

Published by Greenleaf Book Group Press
Austin, Texas
www.gbgpress.com

Distributed by Greenleaf Book Group LLC

For ordering information or special discounts for bulk purchases, please contact Greenleaf Book Group LLC at PO Box 91869, Austin, TX 78709, 512.891.6100.

Design and composition by Greenleaf Book Group LLC and Bumpy Design
Cover design by Greenleaf Book Group LLC

Publisher's Cataloging-In-Publication Data

(Prepared by The Donohue Group, Inc.)
Hiban, Pat.
   6 steps to 7 figures : a real estate professional's guide to building wealth and creating your own destiny / Pat Hiban. — 1st ed.
      p. : ill. ; cm.
   ISBN: 978-1-60832-174-2

   1. Real estate business—Vocational guidance—United States. 2. Real estate business—Economic aspects—United States. 3. Success in business. I. Title. II. Title: Six steps to seven figures
HD1375 .H52 2011

333.33/023/73   2011927132

Part of the Tree Neutral® program, which offsets the number of trees consumed in the production and printing of this book by taking pro-active steps, such as planting trees in direct proportion to the number of trees used: www.treeneutral.com

TreeNeutral®

Printed in the United States of America on acid-free paper

11 12 13 14 15   10 9 8 7 6 5 4 3 2 1

First Edition

This book is dedicated to Howard Brinton

CONTENTS

FOREWORD

Over the years, through various business and book ventures, I've had the privilege of meeting thousands of talented, highly capable, and, in some cases, brilliant real estate sales professionals. Pat Hiban is one of these special people.

Early on in his personal journey, Pat made the decision to lead a success-oriented life. And in twenty years' time he has achieved it in massive fashion—and done it his way. So when he asked me to contribute to a book about his success, I was honored to lend him my support.

Pat Hiban's success is a great story. It amazes me to think of all that he has accomplished. His journey from humble beginnings as a novice salesperson to the number-one sales associate in the nation at ReMax to seventh-level business owner and billion-dollar producer with his Pat Hiban Team at Keller Williams represents something truly special. Pat has reached heights many aspire to yet few dare to attempt and even fewer accomplish.

This book is about Pat's personal pathway to success. It's a story about the big systems, daily practices, and rituals that delivered incredible results and allowed him to live a fulfilling life. Along the way, Pat transitioned from an independent businessperson to a manager of many businesspeople. And he learned how to be successful there too.

You might be reading this book because you're at a transition point yourself. Maybe you want to create a bigger, more successful business; maybe you want to maximize your potential with less effort; or perhaps you just want straightforward tips on how to earn more money. These are all commendable goals, and this book can help you get there.

From the outset of his career, Pat recognized that he was an independent thinker. He knew he was at his best when he was his own boss. He wasn't particularly skilled in any one discipline, nor did he excel at being the best in the classroom or on the sports field. Yet he had the right mind-set, the belief that he could succeed big. That thinking was critical to his success, as were courage, a plan, and big goals. And of course he had the passion for the business.

To fulfill his vision, Pat had to do his homework, ask a lot of questions, and consistently find the right people to help guide him along the way. He worked relentlessly, though he also found the need for balance—something many of us take for granted. He became a true leader and a motivator. And yes, he became enormously successful. Rather than luck, I call it being purposeful. Though he may not have known it then, Pat really was setting out on a quest to create a life worth living and a business worth owning—a vision shared not only by Pat and me, but also by more than 70,000 of our friends at Keller Williams Realty. It brings meaning to what we do every day.

Pat's passion for learning—and for sharing knowledge—is remarkable. He has never stopped asking the right questions, finding the right hires, making the right fires, and implementing the right systems when he has needed them. But ultimately the choice to be great was

Pat's alone. His focus on growth and constant forward motion through purposeful effort paid off. His success, like that of many others, was a success built over many years rather than overnight, and through others, with great effort spent on repeated tasks over time. Pat still brings a passion to the work he does every day. I'd wager that he's teaching scripts or mentoring his employees as you read this now.

In this book you'll find many of the best practical strategies and proven systems that helped propel Pat to mega-agent status. You'll see how Pat was able to climb up and conquer, one step at a time, a long list of carefully planned goals. You can benefit greatly from Pat's practice in affirmations, his diligence, his trials and errors, his experiments, his failures, and his aha's—all of which helped him grow his business and his life potential.

Pat Hiban exemplifies a life carved from purposeful planning and results-oriented action. His journey is one of failing forward, learning, growing, shifting, and rising above the challenges to arrive at a place of immense achievements.

Pat understands the idea of playing an equal-opportunity, unequal-reward game. He practices fundamental business skills better than most and he understands what success means and what it requires in the real estate sales profession.

Candidly I can tell you that he has touched the hearts and minds of many people. Pat has enriched the lives of everyone from clients to co-workers to charitable organizations and, with his wife Kim, has created a beautiful family. Pat has made a positive difference in this world and has been a tremendous success. I'm proud to call him my friend.

To live a truly extraordinary life takes courage. Pat Hiban's desire to be the best is extraordinary too. His efforts and the life he leads continue to inspire me. The writing of this book serves as a testament to Pat's lifelong efforts to achieve greatness. To climb many mountains takes a tremendous belief in ourselves and beyond ourselves—a faith that we can do it, no matter the odds, no matter what life throws at us. When you put this book down, remember that Pat was once like you. He started somewhere and he had a vision of being great and a plan of action to get there. I hope his ideas help you to become the best you can possibly be—wherever you are in your business and your life.

—Gary Keller, bestselling author of *The Millionaire Real Estate Agent*, *The Millionaire Real Estate Investor*, and *Shift: How Top Real Estate Agents Tackle Tough Times*

INTRODUCTION

WHY I'M THE GUY TO SHOW YOU
HOW TO GET TO $1,000,000

About a year ago, I was at a real estate convention in Atlanta, Georgia, for three and a half days. There were probably tens of thousands of attendees. At the end of the first day, I watched from the hotel lobby as a large group of people left to catch a van, on their way to do some after-dinner dancing. I realized all of them had probably eaten already and showered, too. *Funny,* I thought to myself, *it feels as if it were still midday.* I realized I hadn't eaten since breakfast, and I was still carrying my seminar book and free nylon bag with free stuff from the vendors;

I hadn't even made it back to the room to put them down. I looked down at my pocket schedule, where I had circled several different courses offered that day, each of which I had wanted to attend. I hadn't made it to any.

From the moment I set foot in the hotel hallway that connected the seminar rooms, I had talked real estate, nonstop. Now I knew why my wife hated to come to these things. As a seminar presenter, I wore a special name-tag ribbon and a medallion around my neck that made me a target for people who wanted to connect with a top producer. I became a magnet—and I loved it.

Person after person approached me and asked me questions about my real estate business—and theirs. I talked about my days as a beginner all the way up to what I was doing at the time. I was on a natural adrenaline rush. By the end of the day, I had a yellow memo pad full of notes about the newest and latest trends in the market—what was working for everyone else. I realized I had gotten just as many great ideas and information from the dozens of attendees I had met that day as they had gotten from me.

As I lay in bed that night journaling about the day, I realized people really were curious about what I do, and how I do what I do. I think of myself as being modest about my accomplishments, and I used to feel that my last twenty-four years of experience in the real estate business weren't much to talk about. My epiphany that night after the conference was that I was wrong. I guess I really have done something that most people desire to do. I've made millions and not killed myself doing it—and I came from fairly humble beginnings. I took a job that's usually riddled with interruptions, stress, and long hours, and I've made it into one that's fun, funny, and full of free time. I've sold more than a billion dollars' worth of residential real estate—house by house. My average sale price at the start was $91,000, and over the years I've raised it to closer to $450,000. I've had a team as large as fifty-four people and as small as me, myself, and I. I've hired, fired, and been quit on by hundreds of agents and staff members. I've also managed to keep the best ones for more than fifteen years. If there's a way to get sales leads that's out there, I probably not only know about it but also have done it—and probably more than once. I've met thousands of buyers and thousands of sellers, and I've negotiated thousands of contracts. In fact, I've negotiated fourteen different contracts in one day, and I've held on to listings for over two years that never ended up selling.

Most business authors and seminar speakers are just

that: professional authors and speakers. In contrast, I am a working real estate salesperson. As I write this introduction, I am looking at my watch so I won't be late for a meeting with a client. I'm in the fields. I'm on the ground.

In this book, I'm offering a transparent look into my life, my real estate operation, and my day-to-day activities—yesterday and today. I've written it to share with you the lessons I've learned about how to make money in real estate without working too hard. I've been selling real estate successfully for twenty-four years, and for the past sixteen years, I've been building a team of terrific people who have helped my business grow even more.

Twenty-four years ago, when I first started selling real estate, I made only $13,200 a year. I still have that 1099 form tacked to my bulletin board in my office, to keep me humble and to let everyone else in my office know that I started at the bottom. But since then, I've had enormous success in my career: I'm one of the few active real estate agents who have sold more than $1 billion worth of residential real estate, and for two years in a row I sold more than five hundred homes, with gross annual commissions of more than $5 million. Of course, I didn't do that alone: I achieved that success with a team of fifty-four people. That was before the bottom dropped out of the real estate market—but I'm still working, and I'm still successful, because I've found new ways to sell houses and new types of houses to sell.

So how did I get from a yearly rate of $13,200 in commissions to $5 million in commissions? And when the bubble burst, how did I deal with a 65 percent drop in statewide transactions? How did I go from working with no banks on foreclosure properties to working with more than forty, and handling more than three hundred listings for them—in only eighteen months? How can you replicate my success in real estate in your own life? That's what you'll find out in this book.

Because my career and my success have been in real estate, I wrote this book for real estate professionals, although the lessons I've learned about expanding my business are applicable to many other businesses as well. After all, the basics of what I learned were how to manage my own time more effectively and efficiently and how to manage other people better, so that we could all make more money and have more time off—the goals of almost every businessperson. However, my hope is that the information in this book will be especially helpful to real estate professionals of all kinds.

My goal is to show how you can develop a system that will allow you to net a half-million dollars or more while working only four days a week—and while being involved in other money-making activities that are branches of your primary business. I also want to show you how you can create more free time for yourself; I believe it's important to do something besides just working, so you can keep your mind active and not get bored with doing the same old thing, day in and day out.

I've written this book for anyone who wants to "have it all." You want to be rich, but you also want to have balance in your life; you want to have a life outside of work, but you also want to make a lot of money. I think that deep down, everybody really wants that, but only a few really push forward to get it. Maybe you're already successful—either in your company or in your region— and maybe you're even the top-performing person in your office. But maybe you're not *feeling* successful, or maybe you're successful only at work but not in your personal life. If you're feeling out of balance, as though you're working too hard to make money, then this book is also for you.

I believe this book is useful whether you are brand new in the real estate business and looking for a step-by-step process for success or a seasoned real estate pro looking to increase your profits and spend less time working. I hope this book will help you and that you'll return to it again and again for advice: "What did Pat do when this happened to him?"

People ask me all the time why I got into real estate and whether it was because I love houses. Honestly, that wasn't the reason. When I was a kid, I didn't say to myself, "Gee, when I grow up, I want to sell real estate." I was born seventeen months after my older brother, Michael, who was very verbose and active. I, on the other hand, was very slow to develop. I didn't speak until I was five, and my parents took me to a shrink to see if I was just super-shy or actually mute. I was labeled as learning disabled in the first grade and put into special education classes. When I did learn to speak, I mixed up many consonants, the most severe being R and W. I sounded like Elmer Fudd—I said "wabbit" instead of "rabbit"—until close to middle school. In fourth grade I was picked to do the morning announcements, and I was so afraid I wouldn't be able to read them that I purposely walked very slowly on the way to school, dragging my feet until my brother yelled at me and left me in the woods, going on to school by himself. I showed up exactly half an hour late and missed my chance at stardom. I would never have been pegged as a future agent who would master the kitchen-table listing appointment and go on to deliver monologues in several very successful TV commercials.

I was just an average kid, growing up in a single-parent household. My parents divorced when I was twelve, and my mom was a schoolteacher who had to raise all five of us alone. I didn't have any special talents: I wasn't musically gifted, and I certainly wasn't a sports star. I tried out for lots of teams, but I was too uncoordinated to play well—in fact, I was third string on the lacrosse team during my freshman year, and I dropped to fourth string during my sophomore year. I got worse!

I didn't have any strong interest in doing anything in particular, even by the time I went to college. I wasn't a 4.0 student; I graduated with a 2.6 average. I didn't major in anything practical like business or accounting; instead, I majored in sociology because I took many random courses and waited too long to declare a major, and a sociology major required the fewest courses. In other words, I chose it simply so I could graduate on time, with the rest of my class. And when I graduated, I didn't know what the heck I was going to do. All I knew was that

I wanted to make money. My point is that if *I* could become successful—in all ways, financially and emotionally—so can you.

There's a song by the Talking Heads called "Once in a Lifetime" with the lyrics, "and you may ask yourself, 'Well, how did I get here?'" As I asked myself that question over and over again in writing this book, key principles rose to the top. I believe that if you implement all six of these principles and don't give up, it will be literally impossible for you to fail. You will have to succeed.

This book describes what I've learned about real estate sales, about customer follow-up, about managing, motivating, inspiring, and keeping people accountable. It also shares my thought processes on delegating, taking real estate success to the next level, and breaking the workaholic tendencies that many independent businesspeople and small-business owners tend to have. This book is intended to be a guide to making more money, more efficiently, in less time. And who doesn't want that? My hope is that this step-by-step guide will pave the way for you to be more successful in your career. Good luck!

STEP 1

SET GOALS & AFFIRMATIONS: CHANGE YOUR CIRCUMSTANCES IN ONLY FIVE MINUTES A DAY

"People who are unable to motivate themselves must be content with mediocrity, no matter how impressive their other talents."
—Andrew Carnegie

I learned how important it is to set specific goals in my first few years in business, when I attended a terrific seminar given by Floyd Wickman's training and coaching company. The seminar advocated creating a picture of one of your biggest goals, and at that time mine was to buy a townhouse in Columbia, Maryland. So I took a picture of a townhouse, blew it up to 8½" by 11", and wrote on it, "By April 15, I will be able to comfortably buy a nice townhouse in Columbia." I then had the picture laminated and carried it around with me at all times. Today, more than twenty years later, it's crumpled, but I still have it:

I put that picture on my keychain—though because it was so big, I had to keep my keys in my briefcase. It was a constant reminder of my goal, so I couldn't forget or ignore what I was working for, and it worked! I bought my first townhouse right on schedule. And I still own that home today, though I don't live there anymore; now

I rent it out, which brings in additional, passive income every month.

Many people know the story of how Jim Carrey did the same thing with his goals. He started out as a stand-up comedian, then performed on TV's *In Living Color* with the Wayans brothers, then turned to small roles in films. Wanting to make it big, he wrote himself a check for $10 million, because that's what he wanted to be paid some-day for a movie. He dated the check for Thanksgiving 1995 and kept it in his wallet as a constant reminder of his goal. He said he used to drive to a cliff in southern California after he was done working, look out over the city of Los Angeles, and look at this check. In 1996, he was paid $20 million for *The Cable Guy*, at that time a record sum to be paid to a comic actor in a film.

Clearly, having a tangible, written reminder of your goal really works, because it constantly reminds you of what you're striving to achieve.

———

Around the same time that I was beginning to set specific written goals, I also learned the power of making affirmations to myself, and after a few years, I ramped this up by making it a habit. Sometimes I wrote them down; other times I recorded them on CD or cassette and listened to them every day on my way to work. Now I record them on my phone and replay them whenever I get a chance. Ninety percent of the affirmations I've made over the years have come true: Typically, about half come true the year I make them, and the rest come true within five years or so.

Each affirmation is a goal that I phrase as though it *has already happened*, as though I've already achieved it. For example, one of my affirmations when I was just starting out was, "I own a car phone, and I use it a lot." That was a big deal back in the 1980s; there were no cell phones at that time, and car phones cost around $650 and had to be permanently installed in the car, so very few people had them. Nevertheless, I achieved that goal: I bought my car phone the next year. I used it constantly to stay in touch with clients, and it helped my business enormously.

Here's a list of some of my affirmations, with the dates I made them and the dates I achieved them:

AFFIRMATIONS:
GOALS I'VE SET—AND ACHIEVED

Goal	Set/Achieved
"I am an excellent prospector, making cold calls for new business a minimum of two hours per day."	1989/**1990**
"I make more than $105,000 per year."	1990/1991
"I own multiple rental properties."	1990/1994
"I drive a BMW."	1991/1993
"I pay attention to eating healthy. I have a salad with every meal."	1992/1994
"I am the real estate source for the Maryland media."	1993/1996
"I am a $9 million producer."	1994/1995
"I have a high-performance team that is second to none."	1996/2003

"I am a black belt in tae kwon do." (This affirmation changed with every recording as I advanced; at first it was "I am a yellow belt . . .," then six months later it was "I am a green belt . . .," and so on.)	1997/2004
"I awake most mornings at 5:00 a.m. feeling energized and alert."	1997/2005
"My house is paid off."	1999/2002
"Fifty percent of my workdays are dollar productive."	1999/2003
"I am a multimillionaire."	2000/2003
"I take 150 days off per year."	2000/2002
"I sell foreclosures for more than thirty banks and asset management companies."	2008/2010

I realize that some readers may think these affirmations are hokey, or that there's no way they can work. But your subconscious mind is incredibly powerful, and I had a recent experience that reminded me just how powerful it can be.

STEP 1: SET GOALS & AFFIRMATIONS

In the summer of 2008, I went to Tanzania, Africa, with a few other people from Keller Williams Realty to climb to the top of Mount Kilimanjaro. This is one of the "Seven Summits," the seven highest mountains in the world; at over 19,000 feet, Kilimanjaro is the highest in Africa. Three months before I went to Africa, I changed my affirmation CD that I listen to every morning to include a new affirmation: "I am a July 28, 2008, summiter of Mount Kilimanjaro."

That was my goal: to get to the highest point in Africa, where I would be able to see everything below, even the clouds. In fact, I brought with me a red Keller Williams flag, and I planned that when I got to the top, I would take a picture of all of us from KW, waving our flag. The editor of *OutFront*, the Keller Williams magazine, was going to publish the photo in the next issue. I was really looking forward to this trip.

I started training for the climb before I left, but since I live in Maryland, where the altitude is zero, I wasn't prepared for higher altitudes, and there wasn't really any way for me to get ready for them before I left. So I trained physically as much as I could, and when I got to Africa, I took medicine that helped me acclimate to the higher altitude.

For the first four days, I was fine, because we were basically just hiking. But on the last day, we were at 15,000 feet at 5:00 p.m., and we had to go to sleep so we could wake up at 10:00 p.m. and start climbing again at 11:00. Our goal was to get to the summit at 7:00 or 8:00 a.m. and see the sunrise. It was really cold (about 10 degrees Fahrenheit) and very windy, and despite the medicine, I was suffering from severe altitude sickness. Also, there was no social interaction among my fellow climbers. We were climbing basically single file, and our voices were muted by loud winds, so there wasn't anyone I could talk to, no one to help me stay focused and motivated as the climb got more difficult.

By 4:00 a.m., four of our group of thirteen were unable to continue the climb. Some of the porters stayed with them; these climbers would either continue up after resting for a while or decide to go back down. I continued on, but by this time, my water had frozen, so I had nothing to drink, and I couldn't listen to my iPod anymore because I was so bored with all the music I had. So I just said over and over to myself, probably hundreds of times, or maybe even a thousand times: "I am a July 28, 2008, summiter of Mount Kilimanjaro."

I thought everyone would feel as bad as I did, but not everyone did. I wanted to quit, and I asked the group whether anyone wanted to go down with me. But nobody did; the remaining climbers wanted to keep climbing. Part of me wanted to keep climbing, too, but most of me felt so awful that I just wanted to quit.

Then one of the other Keller Williams guys in the group, Mike McCarthy, took my red KW flag out of my backpack and said, "If you're not going to the top, we'll take a picture without you." That made me feel even worse. The other porters began asking me, "What are you going to do? Are you going up or down?" So I said, "Well, let's just take five steps." And then I said, "Let's just take five more steps." And then five more steps. Before I knew it, I was at the top! It almost seemed to me that God had carried me there, because I really don't know how I climbed that extra two hours to the top. Of course, once I got to the top, I felt great.

As I look back on it, I realize that the only thing that got me there was my pumping myself up for three months straight before I left for Africa, and the hundreds or thousands of times that I repeated my affirmation to myself. I truly believe that I made it through those last two hours of climbing only because I repeated over and over, "I am a July 28, 2008, summiter of Mount Kilimanjaro." That was the difference between going forward and *not* going forward.

Me atop Mount Kilimanjaro, 19, 340 feet above sea level.

The point of this story is not that you have to climb Mount Kilimanjaro; you don't even have to *want* to climb Mount Kilimanjaro. But whatever it is that you *do* want to achieve—whether you want to climb a mountain or lead the next space shuttle, or you simply want to be a better employee, a better boss, or a more successful business owner, make more money, or be a better husband or wife or parent or friend—you need only to have the sheer determination to do it. I got to the top of Mount Kilimanjaro by simply climbing five steps at a time. Your goal doesn't have to be something outrageous (although it can be!); all you need to do is keep affirming that this is something you want and something you will achieve, and then keep working toward that goal.

Now that you've read about some of *my* goals, think about your own goals. Take a few moments, pull out a piece of paper, and write down at least one thing you want to achieve in the year ahead. Then rewrite that goal in the present tense, as though you've already achieved it, which will help your mind believe it's possible to achieve. For example, if you make $60,000 a year and want to make $100,000 a year, then your goal would be "I want to make $100,000 per year" and your affirmation would be "I make $100,000 per year." But you can't just throw that out there: As motivational speaker Jim Rohn says, "Affirmation without discipline is the beginning of delusion."

Instead, you have to break down your ultimate goal into smaller goals: You need to specify what daily, weekly, or monthly actions need to take place for you to achieve your goal. Maybe you need two more clients a month.

To get those new clients, you might need to prospect for new clients two more hours a day. So your affirmation would be "I prospect for two additional hours per day."

Or if your goal is to sell five houses priced over $1 million every year, then your affirmation would be "I sell five houses priced over $1 million every year." To achieve that goal, you need to set smaller goals, such as becoming a luxury-home specialist. In order to become a luxury-home specialist, you might say "I prospect for new luxury-home clients every day."

I also believe you should continually set the bar higher, but at the same time understand that sometimes the markets are bigger than you. For example, in 2000, when I met my 1996 goal of having a net worth of $1 million, my affirmation for the next year was "I have a net worth of more than $2 million." At that time, of course, the stock market was growing so fast that you could easily double your portfolio in a year: There were days when I was $50,000 richer at the end of the day, so I thought it would be easy to achieve my financial goal and have $2 million in my retirement account. Then the market crashed, and my million-dollar account plummeted to $350,000 because, like many other people, I had invested heavily in tech stocks and options and other risky investments.

So I was no longer a millionaire, and I certainly didn't make my $2 million goal for that year, which was disheartening. Fortunately, I eventually made back all I had lost in the stock market through my real estate investments.

The key lesson I learned from that experience was that you can be successful in meeting your goals only if you focus your actions on what *you yourself can control*. For example, you need to set goals like "Every day, I will save five dollars" or "Every day, I will make one hundred calls to prospective clients." If you're focusing on how far you have to go, or how bad people are saying the economy is, it's much harder to achieve your goal. Instead, you need to focus on the *actions* you can take, because the market sometimes determines the results—whether it's the stock market, the real estate market, or a consumer market you're selling to. You can't control what others do, so you always have to take the right actions yourself.

Finally, keep the long term in mind when circumstances out of your control prevent you from reaching your target. My investment account did reach $2 million eventually, even though I didn't achieve that goal during the year I'd hoped to achieve it. You might not reach your objective exactly when you want it, but if you keep at it and stay focused, you can achieve it over time. In both investing and business, my advice is the same: *Be patient*, and don't give up. Even if you haven't achieved your target for a particular year, keep reaffirming that goal until you achieve it. Personally, I accomplish about 50 percent of my goals the year I make them. I reaffirm the rest the following year, and if I don't achieve them that year, I reaffirm them the following year. I keep reaffirming a goal until I achieve it. As you set and work toward your goals, you can expect to have the same items on your list for years. They may not come easily, but keep working toward them year after year, and don't give up.

―――

About ten years ago, I attended a seminar led by Dr. Fred Grosse, who spoke at a RE/MAX convention. The essence of his speech was about how to achieve a balance between work and the rest of your life, a subject I'll cover in more detail in Step 6. But he also taught me a new way to achieve my goals. I already knew I could control only my own actions, not the results I was seeking, but Dr. Grosse taught me the value of working with an "accountability partner" or "peer partner"—somebody you team up with and make a commitment to.

Here's how having an accountability partner works: Whether your goal is to lose fifteen pounds in two months or to make cold calls every day between 9:00 a.m. and 11:00 a.m., five days a week, you put it in writing and send it to your partner. Then, at the end of *every day*, you e-mail your partner with an update. For example, if your goal is to do four hours of dollar-productive activity on a particular day, then at the end of the day, you would e-mail your partner with something like this: "Here's everything I did today, and here's how many hours were dollar-productive." ("Dollar-productive" activities are any that *directly* bring money into your business, as opposed to the ancillary activities that many people waste too much time on. I'll describe this in more detail in Step 4.)

I also learned the value of creating both a reward if you do meet your goal and a negative consequence if you don't. For example, your reward could be that if you call your past clients from 9:00 a.m. to 11:00 a.m. every day for the next three months, then at the end of that time, you give yourself a weekend in the Bahamas with your husband or wife. On the other hand, if you *don't* do what you set out to do, then the negative consequence might be to send a check for $5,000 to a political party you don't really want to support. To make sure you follow through, you could give your check to your peer partner as soon as you set the goal, and have him or her mail it if you fail to meet it.

The basic idea of setting rewards and consequences is simple, of course: It's just a carrot and stick. But your peer partner keeps you honest as you use the carrot and stick on yourself. You should e-mail your peer partner *every single day* and let him or her know how you're doing.

Working with a peer partner has worked really well for me and for many other people I've talked to. In fact, I'm still working with the same peer partner I teamed up with more than twelve years ago: David Osborn. We got in the habit of e-mailing each other every day and making commitments twice a year, so we stay in touch with each other and make sure we follow through.

That accountability has been a great asset to my business life, because I've been able not only to set goals but to give them to someone who understands them. I wouldn't be comfortable talking about some of my goals—especially goals related to the amount of money I want to make—to just anyone, especially if my accountability partner didn't earn anywhere near what I'm earning. That's why your partner should really be as much a *peer* as possible: You should be comfortable telling your true goals to him or her.

I have another peer partner now: Tim Rhode, whom I'll tell you more about in Step 6. I met Tim through David, and we later invested in a shopping center together, which was a great investment that has been very profitable for both of us. You never know where a peer-partner relationship will lead!

Another lesson I learned about focusing on my own actions as the primary path to reaching my goals was how important it is to plan my ideal day—and then stick to the plan. The "ideal day" was another idea from Dr. Grosse. Unfortunately, for many people, the ideal day is one where they just show up—and don't have to really do anything at all! In other words, many people are simply reactionary beings; they don't take action like they should.

It's important that you figure out what it is you want to do, so that *you* control your workday rather than merely reacting to the actions of others. There's a book by Julie Morgenstern called *Never Check E-Mail in the Morning* that ties into the same idea: Most people come in to work, and the first thing they do is check their e-mail.

Morgenstern says not to do that; if you do, you're *react-ing* to what people want from you, instead of doing what *you* know you want or need to do. You might think, "Oh, answering a few e-mails doesn't take long," but you're still doing what's important to somebody else, rather than yourself. The next thing you know, an hour and fifteen minutes have gone by and you're behind on the schedule you'd set for the day.

Here's an example of what you *should* do to start your day. Every day, Samina Chowdhury, one of the buyer specialists on my team, writes fifteen handwritten thank-you letters to people she has met—anyone she can think of. She keeps a list of people she's keeping in touch with to try to get referrals from. She does this *before* her e-mails in the morning, and she includes her card as a reminder for them to think of her if they're interested in buying a home. And it works: She consistently gets more referrals than other agents I know. She averages about twenty-five settlements a year from referrals—largely from the people to whom she has sent notes.

So if your ideal day is to get to your office, call previous clients from 9:00 a.m. to 11:00 a.m., and ask them for referrals, then that's exactly what you need to do. Block out the time and don't take any incoming calls or react to anything else. Just follow your plan. After your calls, you might answer e-mails from 11:00 a.m. to 12:00 a.m., take a lunch break, and then meet with any interested sales prospects. No matter what business you're in, plan what *you* want to accomplish each day, do your dollar-productive activities first, and don't let anyone or anything interrupt your plans.

For example, I currently block out every Friday from 9:00 a.m. to 1:00 p.m. to call all my past clients, see how they are, and ask them for referrals. I encourage my agents to do that, too. In addition, every Monday from 2:00 p.m. to 4:00 p.m. in the afternoon, we call all our clients whose homes we're currently trying to sell and give them feedback on what happened over the weekend. We tell them where their properties were advertised, and we give them a status update on any interest from potential buyers. Two days a week, from 2:00 p.m. to 4:00 p.m., I call asset managers of banks and mortgage companies to ask if I can be their foreclosure-listing agent. While I make these calls, I have a virtual assistant listen in and take notes, which allows me to make even more calls during those two hours.

One last point on the subject of goals: You have to set goals that are realistic for the market you're currently working in. And again, you need to realize you can't control everything—such as whether your market goes up or down.

During my first fifteen years in business, I didn't have any problems setting goals and achieving them. When the market changed and our goals just weren't realistic anymore, it was painful. I became discouraged because my team and I had become so accustomed to setting and meeting our goals, and now we weren't. We had been moving and growing so fast for many years:

- In my fifteenth year of doing business, we sold $86 million worth of property;

- in year sixteen, we sold $105 million;

- in year seventeen, we sold $186 million;

- in year eighteen, we sold $203 million;

- in year nineteen, we sold $207 million.

But in year twenty, we did only $145 million. The real estate market had changed dramatically, and we were way off our goal for the year: Based on our success from the two previous years, we had hoped to have another year where we sold over $200 million in real estate. We realized that the real estate market probably would not continue to grow like it had been, but we thought it would at least stay flat. But in real estate, you can go from making money to losing money really quickly—especially if you keep your expenses the same, instead of trimming the fat during lean years.

We had been growing by as much as 80 percent a year, so it seemed as though whatever goal we set, we would be able to achieve and even surpass it. But then the real estate market changed direction, and it became a struggle to meet our goals; they were no longer realistic. That was very depressing because we had set such high goals and I had offered great prizes for the team, but since we couldn't make our goals, there wouldn't be any prizes.

In fact, we used to track everything we did—how many properties we sold, how much commission we earned, and several other factors—but we even stopped doing that because it became too depressing to see how much less we were selling. It didn't matter that it wasn't anyone's fault, that it was just the market that had changed; it still made us feel terrible that business was down and we couldn't meet the goals we had set for the year ahead.

Fortunately, we all learned a valuable lesson from that experience: You have to set realistic goals. And we learned that no one is ever in control of everything.

Unfortunately, the subprime mortgage crisis led to

many foreclosures and flooded the market with properties, and at the same time it seemed the world stopped buying homes. Our business dropped substantially, and that year was tough mentally as well as financially. I had to keep reminding myself that the situation was out of my control. Our first reaction was that there must have been something we could have done to prevent this from happening, something we could have done differently or better; most people can't help but blame themselves. They say, "This is happening because I'm not doing X," or "I hired the wrong people." But that's not realistic. In reality, you're often not in control of what's happening, because so much of work is market-driven. In my particular market, the number of units sold dropped 65 percent over a three-year time frame.

The same thing happened in many other businesses, too: The economy slowed, business was down, and many companies struggled. When that happens, don't beat yourself up. Keep working hard, keep working smart, look for ways to cut costs, and look for new ways you can bring in revenue from other sources. Eventually, the market will bounce back, and you'll be ready to grow again.

YOUR 7-FIGURE GAME PLAN

1. **Set specific goals, write them down, and place the written version where you'll see it often.** You're more likely to achieve your goals if you're constantly reminded of them.

2. **Think positively: Use the power of affirmations to achieve your goals.** State your goals as though they've already come true, as in "I am a millionaire." The words you choose have power over how you think, so if you think negatively—"I'll never get to the next level"—that statement can all too easily come true. But if you state the positive, in the present tense—"I earn $200,000 a year"—that positive statement, too, can easily come true.

3. **Keep working toward your goal, even if it seems unattainable.** Even when it seems like you just can't or won't achieve your goal, don't give up! Keep affirming what you want to achieve, and *keep working toward that goal.*

4. **Find a peer partner to keep you focused and accountable for achieving your goals.** You'll find it

easier to work toward your goals if you know you need to check in regularly with someone else. Make that contact as frequent as possible.

5. **Don't let other people plan your day. Imagine your ideal day—then make it a reality.** Set your own agenda—and stick to it. Don't let e-mail, voice mail, phone calls, or answering to someone else's agenda get in the way of meeting your goals for each day.

6. **Put your goals into daily, weekly, or monthly accomplishable tasks that will get you closer to your big affirmations.** For example, if you want to become a millionaire, you might say "I save $1,000 a month," which is something you can do consistently. Then your peer partner can ask you every month, "Did you put $1,000 in the bank?" That also will help you stay on track.

7. **Finally, make sure you set goals that are realistic for the market you're currently working in.** Remember, you can't control everything—the economy, for example—so don't beat yourself up when things get rough.

STEP 2

TRACK:
THAT WHICH IS MEASURED WILL GROW

"Beware of little expenses. A small leak will sink a great ship."
—Benjamin Franklin

I began this book by emphasizing the importance of setting clear (and written) goals, which I believe is critical to achieving success in any area of your life. It's also critical, however, to keep track of your goals and your progress toward achieving them. Obviously, there's no sense setting a goal, say, to sell a hundred homes and then not keeping track of how many you're selling: You'd never know whether you achieve your objective! You have to set a specific goal, and you have to check how you're doing every day. Then, when you make a sale and get one step closer, you should make a note of that progress.

For example, one of my goals one year was to get one hundred referrals, so I put up a thermometer on my door. Every time I got a referral, I added one line on the thermometer. When I got to one hundred, the thermometer was full. It might sound silly, but you'd be amazed at how compelling such a simple visual device is! You have to have daily accountability to yourself and daily tracking for any goal; you need that constant reminder of your progress. As the old saying goes: out of sight, out of mind. If you're not constantly watching how you're doing, it's too easy to lose sight of your target.

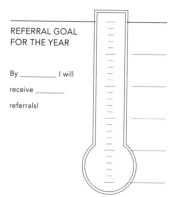

REFERRAL GOAL
FOR THE YEAR

By _____ I will

receive _____

referrals!

STEP 2: TRACK

Here's a list of some of my goals, both professional and personal, for the year ahead.

- I want to be an agent of choice to list foreclosure properties for fifty different banks.
- I want to weigh 170 pounds.
- I want to do yoga at least once a week.
- I want to read twenty-five books.
- I want to add fifty agents to my franchise.
- I want to run a marathon.
- I want to have twelve one-on-one dates with my wife and both daughters.

What are *your* goals for the next year? Whatever they are, I truly believe that you should not only set goals but *look at them as often as possible.* Many people set goals on January 1 but then don't really even think about them during the rest of the year. That's obviously not effective! Instead, you should place reminders in as many places as possible, both at home and at work. Your list of goals could be the screensaver on your computer, or you could laminate them and hang them in the shower, or put them on your car visor—these are all places I've had mine over the years. In fact, during the year I had my goal list on the visor in my car, one of my goals was to make $40,000 a month. And when I took my car to get it inspected, the person who serviced it saw this goal and said, "Man, I want *your* job!" He was also impressed that I kept my list of objectives where I would see it every day.

Keep your list wherever you think you will see it most often, because those constant reminders will help you achieve what you want to achieve.

———

In addition to continually setting and tracking new goals, it's also important to keep track of what percentage of your business comes from what type of client, so you can track where you're growing and where you need to grow.

Only a few years ago, 43 percent of my business came from repeat clients and referrals. I can break that down even further: About 23 percent came from referrals, and about 20 percent came from repeat clients. In fact, we have one client with whom we've worked on twelve property sales. Every time he moves, he hires us, which is terrific. Knowing where this important piece of our business comes from helps us nurture and maintain the relationships that ensure continued success.

STEP 2: TRACK

Our number of referrals will probably increase even more during the next couple of years. In the past, we simply ran television commercials (as described in Step 3). Those ads guaranteed thirty listing appointments a month, and we typically double-ended (represented the buyer and the seller) about 30 to 40 percent of the properties we listed from those ads. But that's just not happening anymore: The tide has turned, and we've definitely moved from a strong seller's market to a strong buyer's market. In a better market, agents were really needed only for the lockbox key, and relationships didn't matter as much. But in a slower market, the relationship with clients matters much more.

In a slower market, buyers (in real estate and many other types of business) will want to hire people who are referred to them. And because most houses in a slower market will be on the market for six months or more, buyers will want to work with an agent who can get them the best deal, fight for them, and negotiate the contract aggressively; they won't want simply to hire a listing agent, who is the seller's agent. In real estate, referrals are important now more than ever. When money is tight, people want to make the best purchasing decisions possible, so they'll rely on good recommendations and references. Real estate professionals who keep track of those types of changes are always ahead of the curve.

Of course, we all have a limited amount of time, so when you have to market more aggressively in a down market, you need to prioritize your time. Because there are really only three types of clients—past clients and their referrals, sphere-of-influence clients and their referrals, and new clients—we prioritize them in the following way:

1. Past clients and people they have referred to us—clients we've worked with in the past who are now interested in buying or selling again and people who have been referred to us. We also call our past clients and ask them, "Who do you know that needs to buy or sell a house in the next six months?"

2. Our sphere of influence—everybody we know and the people they refer to us, including business-to-business relationships such as accountants and lawyers. Again, work your network, and *ask* for new business! For example, if you're on Facebook, your sphere of influence could be all of your Facebook friends, and you could reach out to them through private and public messages.

3. New clients—these are typically people who have called or e-mailed about an ad or a sign they saw or who came to an open house. If you haven't yet met them, follow up and ask them, "Have you bought a house yet?"

When the market is stronger, you need to prioritize differently: Since our referrals may drop, we might ask our past clients if they are interested in moving again. We used to sell many houses to people who were moving up the property scale, whether they were moving from a townhouse or a starter house to a larger family home or from a large house to a very high-end luxury home. We did a lot of this type of sale until recently, because people were trading up: They had good equity in their homes, which they would then use to purchase a nicer home within the same city or region. Now, our focus is on first-time buyers and foreclosures, which is well over 50 percent of our market.

My point is that you need to pay attention to where most of your business and customers are coming from, and then market to those customers to meet their current needs. You can't just keep doing what you've always done. You need to keep up with how your business, the market, and the economy overall are changing—or you won't have any business at all!

It's also important to *pay attention* to and keep track of your own net worth. Whether it's every day, every week, or every month, you should know how much you're worth and how much that has changed during the past week or month. If you're aware of the change, you can use it as a gauge of your success. Step 6 covers saving and investing in more detail, but the point I'm making here is that it's extremely important to *keep track* of how you're doing financially.

For example, I now have my net-worth information on my laptop, so I hit one button that takes me to a spreadsheet that tells me all the properties I own and how much the mortgages were paid down last month. It also links me to the mortgage companies and to my investment accounts, so I can see how much those stocks have gone up or down.

You don't necessarily have to watch this every day, but you do need to be paying attention at least once in a while, on some regular timetable. If you ask most people, "What are you worth?" they won't have a clue. Even very

SMART MONEY TRACKER

MARKETING IDEA	COST	$ MADE	$ LOST	RETURN OF INVESTMENT ($ MADE/LOST + $ SPENT)

I created this as soon as I needed to cut costs. I was spending money on many different things, and I needed a way to take a hard, analytical look at each expense to see if it made sense to continue with it. This tracker allows us to see quickly in black and white whether we need an expense and leaves little room for discussion.

wealthy people often don't know. I think that's ridiculous: If you don't know how much money you have, how can you make it grow?

It's easy to lose sight of your investing goals. To some extent, you don't really have a lot of control over how well your investments do. The first time I realized this was about twelve years ago, when I made this affirmation to myself: "I am a millionaire."

This was when the stock market was going up and

up and up, so it wasn't that unrealistic a goal. I had an account with Merrill Lynch; I checked that account every day, and on February 17, 2000, I saw that it had reached $1,000,040. We celebrated that night at home with cheesesteaks and beer. (We wanted to stay true to how we got to this point in the first place—living below our means and saving money. I'll address this more in Step 6.) Imagine how it feels to be a millionaire. For me it was a large mental security blanket that I began to refer back to in times of stress. I'd say to myself, "I don't care about that; I'm a millionaire." How would your life change if you could say that to yourself each time you worry about something minor?

Millionaires! We celebrated extravagantly—with beer and cheesesteaks at home.

Of course, you should also keep the daily ups and downs of your finances in perspective and make sure you're considering the big picture and your long-term financial goals. Don't get caught up in daily anxiety, and don't overreact to daily changes in the overall economy, the real estate market, or the stock market. For example, during one terrible month of real estate sales, my instant reaction was, *Oh my God, all hands on deck . . . Let's move to a different office space—we have to do* something *immediately to reduce our costs.* And although it's important for anyone in business to be able to reduce costs if they have to, at the same time, it's also important not to overreact.

Sure enough, the very next month, we sold twenty-two properties, and I felt really good compared to how I had felt the month before. I realized that I had over-reacted the previous month when I had started to panic about the state of my business. Unfortunately, it's very easy to overreact when making decisions about your business or your investments, so you need to keep things in perspective. Carefully think through any and all decisions you make, instead of just acting impulsively during a down market.

Another reason to track how well you're doing (in your business or your investments) is because when the market turns, it can turn very fast. For example, it was in 2007 that our business started to turn, because real estate in general had hit bottom. I came to the office one day, and there was a chart on my desk that Olu, my accountant, had left for me. I looked at this report, which showed that in September of the previous year we had settled forty-one homes. But during September a year later, with the same expenses and the same team, we had settled only *six* houses! That was an enormous decrease from one year to the next.

Moreover, the problem with real estate is that *you're only as good as your last sale*—in contrast to other businesses, where you have regular clients. So you can never really look out and plan a year ahead of time: In real estate, we can look out only sixty days, sometimes only thirty. When most businesses go down, they go down only 10 percent or so, which isn't great. But we dropped *85 percent*—a huge loss. Our expenses were still $250,000 per month, which had been okay when we were supporting forty-one settlements. But with only six settlements, all my staff, equipment, and other costs became hugely expensive. In fact, I could do that much business on my own, with no team at all!

So what was I going to do? I had built and built and

built my business, and a few years ago, I realized I had to start tearing it down and scaling back.

Should I have seen this coming? Definitely. The signs were there, but I didn't see them. I'm in good company: Most Americans didn't foresee what happened to the economy. Still, we all need to be more vigilant. When you see that something is working, great—react as though you're at a green light, and *go go go go*! But when something is not working, you need to red-light it to protect yourself.

To some extent, I've been successful in my business not only because I've worked hard, but also because I've been lucky. For a consistent five years, the real estate market was really booming—and five years is a long enough time to make you feel that the success will last forever. And obviously, it's easier to be successful when your industry is on the rise. But even if your industry is solid, you still need to work hard and be smart about how you spend your time and how you grow your business. Especially in a down market, you have to be even savvier so that you don't lose what you've worked so hard to build.

The first thing you need to do is to pay attention to what's selling well in the market you're currently doing business in. I relearned this lesson a few years ago when I ran into Tim Harris, founder of Harris Real Estate University with his wife Julie. I originally met Tim at a real estate mastermind conference, but I hadn't seen him in about five years. We were talking about my business, and I told him my sales were down. He diagnosed my problem by saying, "You need to go to where the money is flowing *now*. Business is like riding the waves when you're surfing—for instance, in the cell phone industry, a lot of people got really rich really fast because they rode that wave when it took off. And the same thing happened with cable TV. But because fewer and fewer people are buying houses now, you're not going where the money is flowing." Then he asked me, "Where do you think the money is flowing? Could your expertise be put to use in any of those areas?"

Obviously, a lot of people were having trouble with their real estate following the real estate crisis of 2007. As we all know from watching the news, a lot of people were either short-selling or in foreclosure. When I was talking with Tim at the conference, I knew that the foreclosure business was going to be big—at least in my area, in Maryland. As Tim had pointed out, I needed to go where the money was flowing, and I realized that made a lot of sense.

So I came back and made a plan to get into the foreclosure business. I started prospecting to people who I knew might be able to get me into that field, and I started letting people know that this was what I wanted to do.

For example, my wife and I were out to dinner one night, and we ran into an appraiser I know who works for Wells Fargo. I asked him who at Wells Fargo does foreclosures, and he told me he would check. I followed up a few days later, and eventually he gave me a name. I immediately sent a package of information about my business to that person.

You need to do the same thing: Find out where the money is, right now. Then, find a way to get into that part of the business. Work your network, find people who will be willing to help you, and then work steadily and proactively to grow.

In addition to tracking the real estate market to follow where it was going, I also continued to track my business's expenses. The first thing we found was that advertising has a point of diminishing returns: We advertised in a lot of papers every week, and we found that if we changed our frequency to every other week, consumers didn't even notice. After all, if you're well known and have a familiar brand, you don't need to advertise every week. So we cut our advertising costs in half, and we noticed no change in our business. Advertising every other week didn't mean that fewer people called us to list their houses.

We also had two billboards that cost $5,000 per month each (which I mention again in Step 3), but they weren't working for us at all. Since we hadn't seen any increase in calls because of these billboards, we stopped using them very early on.

We also removed all of the brochure boxes from our "for sale" signs, which saved us money in several ways. First, we saved money by not printing the expensive color fliers that used to fill those boxes. Many of these fliers were taken by neighbors and other passersby who were just curious about the price of the homes. We saved about $3,000 per month in color toner alone when we stopped producing and replacing them. Second, we figured that creating, printing, and distributing these fliers was about 30 to 40 percent of one person's job, so we eliminated the expense of her time as well.

Also, not printing and distributing these fliers actually *increased* leads: Because we weren't giving out information at the "for sale" sign, people who were interested in a particular property *had* to call us to get information if they were seriously interested in seeing it. Now, they call in and are directed to an agent who will follow up with them.

We also cut our postage bill massively in an effort to cut our costs. In 2006, I spent close to $12,000 mailing out calendars at the end of the year. When the market slowed, we took a list of four thousand and cut it down to my top two hundred. Instead of mailing randomly to every person I'd come into contact with since the beginning of my career, I decided to scrub the list down to only people who had given me referrals during the past two years. I gave the other 3,800 names and addresses back to my agents and said, "Who on this list either bought a house from you or gave you a direct referral recently? Put them on your list and mail them a calendar." The agents are now responsible for mailing their own calendars. That way, they are taking the risk and paying for their own marketing, but I still benefit if the agent makes a sale.

Over the years, I've found that some items work better than others in terms of keeping our business's name in front of clients. Here are my top six items of value that should be mailed out to people (other than postcards, which are a different type of marketing):

1. Magnetic business cards. These are the best things you can mail out. They're inexpensive to create, and they don't cost much to send through the post office. You can buy them wherever you can buy a blank magnet. Once you have the magnet, just stick your business card on it. People use them on their refrigerators, and they stay there for years, holding up their kids' report cards, memos, pictures, etc. Magnetic business cards are worth their weight in gold.

2. Calendars. As mentioned, we mail out calendars every year because people love them; after all, they're very useful. Magnetic calendars are best, because people can stick them to their fridges or file cabinets. They're a great advertisement for your business; again, you're putting your name in front of people every time they look at the calendar to schedule something.

3. Cookies. We used to send out gift certificates for giant cookies on a client's birthday—they were almost like cakes, where you could write messages via the icing. We now just send them out on the first anniversary of their settlements (another cost-cutting measure—one anniversary versus several birthdays). This is another inexpensive way of staying in touch: Giant cookies cost only about $13 each, you can get them at almost any local mall, and people love them. They're an unexpected treat.

4. A list of recommended vendors. We have gotten a great response from sending out a list of trustworthy vendors, including plumbers, handymen, and other home maintenance professionals. People love getting these because the information is more useful than looking in the yellow pages; since you're *recommending* these vendors, your clients don't have to worry that they'll call someone at random and get terrible service. Plus, you can send an updated list once a year, and clients really appreciate that information.

5. A reminder that we offer notary services. Most of my agents are also notaries, and we offer this service for free. We've found advertising this to customers very useful. We might not have heard from a customer in many years, but when that person needs something, he or she will remember that we're all notaries, and it's a way we can stay that person's real estate agent for life.

6. Community participation invitation. Each year I like to give back to the community in some way, and one way that's quite easy is a blood drive. The Red Cross will help you set the entire thing up, and they'll even help advertise it for you! A few weeks prior to our event, we send a postcard out to our mailing lists to invite them to participate. This serves as one more way to make contact with your sphere of influence and past clients, and also allows you to be a force for good in your town. Whether it's a blood drive, a coat drive, a Habitat for Humanity build, or another community service activity, invite everyone you know to be part of the giving!

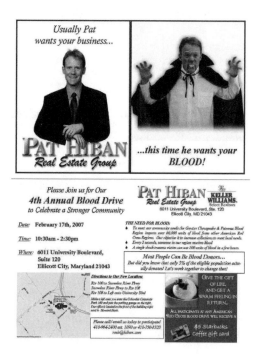

—YOUR 7-FIGURE GAME PLAN ——

1. **Keep track of your goals and your progress toward achieving them.** If you don't keep track of your goals, you'll never know whether you achieved them! Keeping track can be as simple as writing in a notebook or drawing a thermometer on your wall, and the advantage of having a visual reminder in front of you at all times is that *there's no way you'll forget that goal.*

2. **Know where your business is coming from now.** Don't just do what you've always done; keep up with how your business, the market, and the economy overall are changing—or you won't have any business at all! As my colleague Tim Harris advised, *go where the money is flowing.*

3. **Keep track of your own net worth.** You should know how much you're worth and how much that has changed since the last time you checked. If you don't know where you stand, how can you make sure you're going where you want to be? Use the variation in your net worth as a gauge of your success.

GOAL SHEET

Yearly Income Goal $ _____

Average Commission Buyers $ _____

Average Commission Sellers $ _____

Of Vacation Weeks   _____

Of Work Weeks   _____

	Listings Taken	Sales	Seller Commission	Buyer Commission	Total
Jan	_____	_____	_____	_____	_____
Feb	_____	_____	_____	_____	_____
Mar	_____	_____	_____	_____	_____
Apr	_____	_____	_____	_____	_____
May	_____	_____	_____	_____	_____
June	_____	_____	_____	_____	_____
July	_____	_____	_____	_____	_____
Aug	_____	_____	_____	_____	_____
Sept	_____	_____	_____	_____	_____
Oct	_____	_____	_____	_____	_____
Nov	_____	_____	_____	_____	_____
Dec	_____	_____	_____	_____	_____

*MONTHLY totals should equal INCOME GOAL.

*WEEKLY goals should be based on 52 weeks, less # OF VACATION WEEKS

1. Avg. Commission Buyers $ _____

2. Avg. Commission Sellers $_____

3. Yearly # of Buyer Appts Needed   _____

4. Yearly # of List Appts Needed   _____

5. Monthly # of Buyer Appts Needed   _____

6. Monthly # of List Appts Needed   _____

My agents fill out this goal sheet every year. It helps them realize what their aspirations are and what needs to happen to reach their goals. If they know that in order to sell two listings per month they need to go on one listing appointment per week, and a week goes by without an appointment, then they know they are falling off track.

4. **As you track, make sure you're considering the big picture.** Don't get anxious, and don't overreact to daily changes in the overall economy, the real estate market, or the stock market. Instead, plan for the long term, not the day-to-day ups and downs.

5. **Keep your eye on the real prize: how much money you're earning.** Don't get caught up in how you rank against other salespeople or your competitors, in either your region or your own office. Instead, focus on attaining your own personal best. And focus only on the bottom line: how much money you made for yourself and for your company, after your expenses. *That's* what pays your bills.

6. **Watch your expenses.** When you're doing well, it's easy to spend money, but don't let your spending get out of control. Know where your money is going and what you really need to do business, so if your business shrinks a bit—as every business does from time to time—you'll know right away what you can cut back on.

STEP 3

FIND MENTORS & MASTERMINDS:
LEARN FROM THE BEST AND
COPY YOUR WAY TO SUCCESS

"Imitation is the sincerest flattery."
—C. C. Colton

"Sit in the corner and do what you're told" is one of the most important lessons I've learned in my career, and believe it or not, it has helped me become as successful as I am. Most businesspeople don't want to sit in the corner and be told what to do—especially if they're eager to make a lot of money and be successful, as I was more than twenty years ago when I was just starting out. This certainly doesn't *sound* like good advice for overachievers, right?

Wrong.

Too many people think they're smarter than everyone around them, smarter than the people who have been working in that company and industry for many years and have knowledge and experience that others can learn from. I'm not suggesting that you should imitate *everyone* around you; instead, find the most successful person in your office, figure out what he or she is doing right—and then do exactly that.

You don't have to do something new to be successful in business. Success frequently comes from copying the successful practices of other people. The first and most important part of copying your way to success is the mentor-mentee relationship. For my whole life, I have strived to be on both ends of this relationship: I'm constantly reaching out in both directions.

I learned this from Howard Brinton, one of the many seminar leaders I've heard over the years. Howard is the founder of Star Power, a top real estate education company, and he runs mastermind conferences, where like-minded people share their ideas, best practices, and systems of success. I've gone to many of his and other mastermind conferences, where I've met real estate agents who were doing a lot of business and who gave me ideas that I also used successfully. Howard taught me that you don't have to reinvent the wheel when you're trying to do something you've never done before; chances are, there's someone else—maybe not in your town, but somewhere—who has already done what you want to do. Moreover, that person is probably doing it better and more efficiently than you, so you need to find him or her, whether through networking groups, the Internet, or some other means. Once you find that person, don't be afraid to talk to him or her, and don't be afraid to copy what he or she is doing.

I did exactly that at my very first job, when I went to work for Grempler Realty. As I mentioned in the introduction, I graduated from college with a degree in sociology, which didn't leave me with many viable work options. All I knew was that I was hungry to make money, because we didn't have a lot of money when I was growing up. My parents were divorced, and my mom raised me and my four siblings on her own. We weren't poor, but we weren't rich, either. I didn't want to have to worry about money, and I had heard there was money to be made in real estate.

So I took the real estate test, passed, and got a job at Grempler Realty, which often hired people with no experience, as long as they were willing to learn and willing to work—and I was. I quit substitute teaching so I could focus on my new job fulltime.

The Grempler office was set up like a big bullpen: All of the desks were crammed together in clusters of tiny cubicles. I was given a desk between two blonde women in their forties who had big bouffant hair and smoked incessantly (back then, you could still smoke in offices). All day long, they smoked and talked as they sat at their desks and waited for the phone to ring. That was the way many real estate agents worked at that time: They simply waited for potential buyers and sellers to call.

Anyway, after a few weeks, I asked to be relocated to the back of the room, because I have asthma and I didn't want to be sandwiched between the two smokers. Even though I was new, the manager acquiesced to my request because I was one of the only full-time agents; the other agents worked only occasionally, whereas I was giving this job all of my time and effort. My new desk was next to a guy named Erv Norgren, who is a friend to this day. Erv was a top producer, so he had his own private office in the back, separate from the bullpen where everyone else had to sit. Because I had asthma, I got lucky and was placed next to him, and he was nice enough to let me share his office.

Erv was a military guy on reserve duty; he had retired a few years earlier as a colonel. He was also incredibly successful at buying and selling real estate. Most people didn't know that Erv was extremely wealthy and owned more real estate than probably anybody else in the area. He was the Donald Trump of Howard County, Maryland. Nobody knew this because he was quiet and kept to himself, and he didn't look like he was wealthy. He never wore dressy clothes, and he wasn't flashy; instead, he was mild-mannered, a "millionaire next door" type— a low-key guy who drove an ordinary car and lived in an ordinary house and didn't flaunt his wealth. In fact, Erv lived in a house that was smaller than his rental properties. He was just a regular guy who lived modestly, not ostentatiously.

Erv always brought a bologna-and-cheese sandwich for lunch, and once I moved to the desk next to him, he began offering me half every day. I always took it, and he loved that I took it. That was how Erv became my first mentor. He taught me that I needed to go out and get business, that I needed to be proactive, that I needed to put blinders on and not be distracted by all the socializing in the office, and that I needed to get to work. He pointed out that the bouffant ladies were reactive, whereas he was *proactive*.

Erv showed me a better way to work, a way that had worked for him, and I paid attention because he clearly was so successful at selling real estate. He taught me that waiting for business was for the low producers; in contrast, high producers went out and *got* business. What I learned from Erv was his discipline: He came to the office every day and performed consistently, whereas other real estate agents just showed up sporadically. And he always arrived on time. He was punctual, and he worked steadily, diligently, and methodically throughout the day. It may sound simple, but those traits were the keys to his success.

Erv also treated every lead that came in as if it were a potential commission. He showed me that just because a client wasn't a referral or a family member or a friend, it didn't mean that that lead was not just as valuable. Erv represented some builders, and he held open houses for the model homes. He let me sit in on some of those open houses, and he told me that if I met people who were looking for a house, I should follow up with them and treat them like commissions. And I got business that way.

Erv also gave me leads: He had pages and pages of names of people who had come to his open houses. He had called them back, but they hadn't responded to him, so he gave them to me to follow up on. I called every person he gave me and asked one simple question: "You came by three months ago—have you bought a house yet?"

And I got clients! Just as easy as that.

This simple question worked so well because most agents would call prospects and ask, "Hey, how's it going? Do you remember coming by the open house? Do you have an agent?"

Those questions don't work. It's too easy for people to duck them and just say they don't remember or they're not interested. But "Have you bought a house yet?" is a straightforward question, and the answer is either yes or no. And if the answer was no, that gave me a great lead-in to the next question: "Why not?" As soon as I got that no, I'd know I had a prospective customer, so I'd put a star next to that name. I'd say, "Let me see if I can help you," and go from there.

Erv taught me to do that, and it was a very valuable lesson. Again, it may sound simple, but it was very effective: It helped me increase my income substantially. In my first year at Grempler, I made only $13,730 in commissions, mostly because my father let me sell his condo for him, which led to a few more condo sales, and because I sold a couple of mobile homes. That was enough to live on then; my rent was only $300 a month and I had a twenty-year-old Toyota Celica that was paid off. But I couldn't live on that kind of money forever, and Erv's advice helped me to double my income the following year. (Also, that Celica had only two doors, and most real estate agents say you need to have a car with four doors. But I made it work until I could afford something better.)

I got lucky by being assigned the desk next to Erv; it was almost accidental that I found such a terrific mentor. But you don't have to wait for providence to give you a mentor: Look for the person in your workplace who has been successful, spend time with that person, and follow his or her lead. There's always *someone* who knows more than you do—even if only because that person has been in real estate longer than you have. Find that person and learn how he or she became successful.

Here's another example of how I "copied" my way to success by seeking out and learning from mentors.

Around 2001, I decided I needed a new way to advertise and promote my business. I had heard that an agent in Arizona named Russell Shaw was doing television commercials—and that they were working. I had never done TV commercials before; up until that time, I had found clients primarily by cold-calling, taking calls from buyers and sellers, networking and getting referrals, holding open houses, and mailing out postcards and fliers. (I didn't even do billboard advertising until one year when we were really flush. I decided to try them and spent $5,000 a month on two billboards for an entire year, but we found that that approach wasn't successful. We got only three listing appointments and one listing from the two billboards.)

After I heard about Russell's success, I realized that TV was a way for me to get in front of *thousands* of people instead of just calling one person at a time. I decided to give it a try. I cold-called Russell and asked him for advice on what I should say, how I should say it, what he thought worked, etc. I explained that I sell properties only in Maryland, and that because he was working in a different geographical market (Phoenix), we obviously weren't competitors. He soon realized he had nothing to lose by helping me out.

Russell essentially wrote my script for me; he encouraged me to use his pitch verbatim. That was great news to me: I knew he was much more experienced in marketing his business through TV commercials than I was, and I figured that if these ads worked for him, they should work for me, too. Russell not only helped me write my commercial, but he also helped me rehearse the script on the phone before I actually shot and produced it. The only change I made was to shoot my commercials outdoors to take advantage of natural light, whereas Russell shot his commercials in his office. (You can see some of my commercials on YouTube, at www.youtube.com/pathiban.)

My results were even better than his results (and his commercials had been incredibly successful): We made $4 for every $1 we spent. Here are the figures for our best year of running TV commercials:

- We spent $159,642 on producing and running the commercials (the production cost only a few thousand dollars; the rest, of course, was the airtime).

- We sold sixty-six properties that year because of our TV ads, which resulted in $574,200 in commissions.

- We represented eight buyers who called because they saw our TV commercials, which brought in another $69,600 in buyers' commissions.
- The total earned was $643,800, which is about four times what we paid out.

That's a *great* return. We figure that getting any return on our marketing dollars that's even close to a 2:1 ratio—meaning that we get $2 back for every $1 we spend—is beautiful. And this was a 4:1 ratio, which is very hard to achieve in this business. We knew that this commission money came directly from the TV commercials because we asked everybody who called us during that time frame what prompted them to get in touch with us. Just as I had hoped, what had worked for Russell worked for me, too—and all I had to do was call him and ask him to share what he had done in his market, which he was happy to do.

Moreover, these figures don't even include the indirect profit we made from these commercials. We got additional buyers and sellers from the ads and signs, plus we got great name recognition from having all these listings. So, in addition to making almost $650,000 in commissions from the *direct* sales we got because of the TV commercials, we probably made another $1 million *indirectly* from sellers who called in after they received our "just sold" postcards or saw our "sold" signs in front of the sixty-six homes we sold from the TV commercials that year. Plus, we procured at least another half-million on buyer sales from buyers we met at open houses, or from calling on the signs of those 66 homes. It was a great snowball effect that led to lots of new business.

One piece of advice I share with other people who want to do their own TV commercials is that most people (unless they're actors) are very uncomfortable and stiff in front of the camera. Consumers will react to your body language more than to what you're saying. So I smiled *constantly* on my first TV commercials, and I still do that today. The producer brings jokes with him and makes me laugh, and then they start shooting me while I'm laughing, and it makes a huge difference.

Many people have even called me and said, "I don't know what it is about your commercials, but my kids love you, they repeat the words you say, and they know your name. They tell me, 'You better call Pat Hiban when it's time to sell our house.'" I work really hard to come across as approachable and friendly, and kids respond to that—even more than their parents do. But their parents sure notice when the kids tell them to call me! So we've gotten lots of business from TV—and I have Russell Shaw to thank for that, because he helped me copy what he was doing in his market, and it worked just as well for me as it had for him.

If you're reading this and thinking, *I don't have $160,000 to spend on advertising on TV!* I get it. But that's not my point. My point is that there's someone out there who's already doing what you should be doing based on your budget, and you can probably contact that person and simply ask for help. Many times, more often than you probably expect, that person will be happy to help you, as long as you aren't in direct competition.

———

I've also borrowed great ideas from other real estate agents, and they've worked for me, too. A few years ago I met Judy Markowitz, an agent who works in New York City, in Flushing, Queens. I met her at a seminar taught by Howard Brinton, and while we were talking about how we find new clients, she showed me some postcards she had done. Lots of real estate agents use postcards, but

Judy's were really clever. For example, one repurposed a picture of her daughter hanging upside down from a jungle gym, with her hair falling down toward the ground. Judy had turned the picture upside down so her daughter's hair appeared to be standing straight up and added the caption "Is selling your home a hair-raising experience?" and a simple suggestion: "Call Judy today."

Judy sent me samples of all the postcards she had sent out for the previous two years, and I simply retook the pictures and copied her ideas—with her permission, of course. Again, because she was working in a completely different region, she had no problem with my using her ideas. I put a slightly different spin on mine, of course. I didn't use a picture of Judy's daughter on my postcards; I used my two daughters instead (and they got a kick out of that!). The basic ideas were the same; I just changed some of the details. The next pages show some of my versions.

I've found that most people don't mind sharing their ideas. As the old saying goes, imitation is the sincerest form of flattery, and both Russell and Judy were pleased to have done something so well and so successfully that another agent from a different region of the country had found out about it and wanted to borrow their ideas.

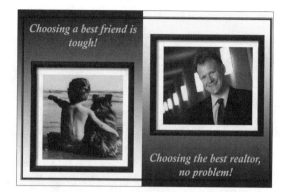

And I'm the same way: If everyone who reads this book were to use a version of the postcards I've shown here, I would have no problem with that, so feel free! My basic attitude about work is an *abundance* mentality. I don't mind if other people use my ideas, because I believe in sharing all my ideas and materials. People call me all the time and ask for a disk with my commercials on it, which is why we simply put them on YouTube. They're now easier to find—and copy. If you want to borrow our ideas, feel free to take a look at our websites, www.hiban .com and www.pathiban.com.

There's no time limit to copying something successful. Many people fear that if someone else in their market is already doing something, then it's too late for them to do the same thing. They worry that their customers will know they're copying that idea from the first person who implemented it. They think, *Oh, this has already been done, so we have to come up with something fresh and new and original.* But I've found that's not true at all.

For example, several years ago, we heard about the idea of offering our clients free access to trucks they could drive to move their belongings. So we bought two sixteen-foot box trucks from U-Haul, pictured here. You don't need a commercial truck driver's license to drive this size truck, so it was perfect for people who wanted to move their own households rather than hire a more expensive professional moving service.

I had heard about the idea of offering this service about ten years earlier, again from an agent in another state, and I realized it was a great additional service we could offer to our clients. Plus, with "Pat Hiban Real Estate Group" on the side of the truck, it's a great advertisement, like a moving billboard for the company. So I negotiated the deal to buy the trucks, and I figured out all the details of how we would lend them to our clients and track who had which truck for how long. Right after I completed the deal, I found out that another agent in my area had just done the same thing: She had her own moving trucks, with *her* name on the side. For a few days, I was really in a dilemma. I worried that I couldn't offer my moving trucks because everyone would think I copied her, especially since she was located so close to our offices. But since all the arrangements had been made, I decided to go ahead and do it anyway. And it wasn't a big deal: None of my clients cared that someone else was doing the same thing; they were just happy we offered the service.

Now, of course, there are plenty of real estate agents with moving trucks in my region. We all offer this service, so it's no longer something special that differentiates us, but it's still a valuable service. There was no reason not to implement it just because someone else already had. Think about your own business and what additional services you could offer to your customers or clients, even if one of your competitors is already offering that service. In some cases, it's best to be first to market because you capture people's attention and have the advantage of originality. On the other hand, sometimes it's best to be second to market, because somebody else has already done all the work to pave the way for the new product or service. As the second adopter, you can be early on the curve but also follow their path.

———————

I've continued to copy my way to success, to learn new ways to sell real estate even since the bottom dropped out of the market. This is what *everyone* needs to do, in real estate and in any other business. When your market or the economy changes, you need to change the way you do business. The first thing to consider is whether there's still a need at all for the product or service you're offering. In real estate, people will continue to buy and sell houses; the prices will just drop. Also, there has been a huge increase in foreclosures and short sales, which I didn't really know anything about when the market crashed—no one did, because they were very rare until 2007. So in keeping with my idea of always following the money, I knew I needed to learn about the foreclosure business.

Back in 2002, I met an agent named Chantel Ray, who sells real estate in Virginia Beach, at one of Howard Britton's Star Power conferences. Shortly after the conference, Chantel called and asked me to coach her on how she could increase her business, because at that time, I was doing five hundred settlements a year. I coached her, and her business did increase. Then, when my business dropped, I found out she was doing even better than

I was; I asked her what she was doing differently, and she said she was selling foreclosures. She had two hundred foreclosure listings, and I didn't have any. Now it was my turn to ask her if she would coach me.

I asked her if we could talk every week, and she agreed. We talked every Monday for about thirty minutes, and our calls continued for six months or so. She gave me an incredibly generous gift of her time, and I hope to be able to pay her back in some way.

I did exactly what Chantel told me to do. She told me I needed to go online and fill out forms for every bank and asset management company I could find. So I filled out all the applications and called each of those banks. Because it was cumbersome and time-consuming to fill out all of those forms (it took about forty-five minutes for each one), I asked her how she did it, hoping that I could use my own time more efficiently. She told me she used a virtual assistant and gave me her number. I hired that person to fill out the forms for me, too. Chantel also taught me the best ways to follow up with these banks, and again, I did exactly what she suggested.

The results have been terrific: Within eighteen months, I went from zero banks and zero foreclosure listings to thirty-two different banks that give me business, and I have 320 foreclosure listings today. In fact, I have accounts with some banks that even Chantel doesn't have, so I'm helping her connect with some of those banks so she can further expand in her market. The system I learned from Chantel is working, and it's 100 percent the result of her mentoring and my belief in learning and copying.

If your business has changed, first figure out what is different and how *you* need to change in order to survive and thrive. Then find someone who has made that change successfully, and ask him or her for help. Mastermind conferences and seminars attended by like-minded professionals are a great place to meet these people. You'll find that many people are very willing and happy to help you, so don't be afraid to ask. It will be your job to do what they tell you to do without letting pride or fear or any other negative emotion get in your way.

After I got into the foreclosure business with Chantel's help, I wanted to expand my network even further in this new aspect of the real estate industry. So I joined the Elite REO network, which is a mastermind organization consisting of REO agents only. (REO stands for "real estate owned," which refers to property that has been foreclosed on by a bank.) Through referrals from agents I've met in the Elite REO mastermind network,

I've gotten four very large accounts. One account immediately gave me fifty homes to sell.

I've even gotten some accounts by mentioning my listings on my Facebook page. Agents have responded by asking me if I have a particular account, and then I've started communicating with those agents and finding new business. That's the power of networking: I have six thousand friends on Facebook (believe it or not!) because I realize the value of social networking, and I've worked to expand my network of friends, colleagues, customers, and friends of friends.

I got another big account through Chris Cormack, an agent in Virginia whom I met through the Keller Williams network. Keller Williams has a mastermind conference every three months, during which you can fly to Texas (where the company is headquartered) and mastermind with other people who are doing work similar to yours. It's a great opportunity to get new ideas from other successful people.

In *Think and Grow Rich*, Napoleon Hill wrote that there are two reasons people don't succeed. The first is that they don't mastermind with other people who are doing the right things, and the second is that they give up too soon. Don't let either of those happen to you.

Whatever business you're in, you need to keep up with new ways of networking, marketing yourself, and doing business. Work isn't stagnant; it's ever-changing, and if you don't know how to do something new, just ask someone else who does, and then do exactly what they recommend.

———

The other aspect of this type of relationship is that when *you* can help someone else by being a mentor, you should jump at the chance. It's good karma, and it's good business. Throughout my career, I've worked hard to find mentors, and I've always agreed to mentor others when asked.

I was recently reminded of how important it is to give back when one of my friends died of kidney cancer at only forty-nine years old. Ken Hovet was a lawyer who loved football so much that he gave up his law practice to become a social studies teacher and high school football coach. At his funeral, there were at least fifty men he had coached over the years, most of whom he had kept in touch with and continued to mentor into their adulthood. Many of them were openly crying at the loss of their friend and mentor. As I mourned my friend, I was simultaneously happy that his legacy would live on in these men, and I realized that every mentee a person has brings an opportunity for immortality. I hope that after I'm gone, whatever I've taught my own mentees or however I've helped them will live on in them, and I hope all my mentees pass something on to their own mentees.

Sometimes your mentees can help you, too, in unexpected ways down the road. For example, one of my mentees is Mark Schwaiger, who graduated from the same college I did a few years after me and belonged to the same fraternity that I did. I met him when I was twenty-four years old, during homecoming weekend at my alma mater. At the time Mark was a fraternity pledge. Mark and I were talking when I had to cut the conversation short to work a real estate deal. Because my college was in the mountains, the cell phone reception was poor, and I was going to drive to the top of the mountain to use my phone. Mark asked if he could come with me. He sat and listened while I negotiated the deal, with back-and-forth calls to the potential buyer and the other agent. I'm sure other frat brothers might have asked Mark to detail their car while they were on the phone, but I was impressed that he wanted to listen to me conducting business so he could learn how I had become successful in only a few years out of college. We stayed in touch over the years, and I became a mentor to him.

Today, twenty years later, I'm still a mentor to Mark, but he has also helped me out. Mark worked in the payroll business for many years, and finally he decided to open his own business. Because he didn't have enough capital to start it, I helped him fund the operation, and now his payroll company is very successful. He runs five thousand payroll checks every two weeks for many small businesses. I own 20 percent of his company, so I get a profit distribution check for $2,500 each month—more passive income. My point is that although mentoring is primarily about helping others, your mentees can help you, too!

This has happened to me twice now. I also own 10 percent of a software company that another mentee of mine, Jason Jannati, started. The reality is that if someone reviews goals with you every year and one of those goals is to open a company, who do you think will be the first person to know about it and have the opportunity to invest in it?

Right! The mentor—you.

If you aren't ready to be a mentor and are looking for a mentor yourself, try to find someone who meets these four criteria:

1. Someone who has success in the area, position, or industry you're working in or interested in.

2. Someone you're not afraid to talk to, and who's not judgmental.

3. Someone who's interested in being a mentor. Obviously, if the person isn't really interested in helping you, he or she won't be all that helpful.

4. Someone who challenges you, who won't let you slide on things, and who will follow up with you to make sure you're achieving the goals you've set for yourself.

In the beginning, you want to reach out and find a mentor, and then several mentors. But as you get older and more experienced and successful in your career, you can have many more mentees than you did mentors. I've benefited from all my mentor and mentee relationships, and I'm confident that mentoring can help you in your career, too.

— YOUR 7-FIGURE GAME PLAN —

1. **When you're trying something new, find some-one who has already done it successfully, and use what you learn from them.** Most people are happy to share their ideas with others, as long as you're not competing directly with them. Why reinvent the wheel when you don't have to?

2. **Keep in mind that you don't have to be first at something to be successful.** Let someone else pave the way and break new ground, then follow in their footsteps. The moving trucks we offered as a service to our clients were no different from other real estate agents' moving trucks, but our clients appreciated them all the same, and they were a great moving advertisement for our company. You don't have to be unique in what you do; you only need to be effective and provide a valuable service to your clients.

3. **Seek out tools and resources that you can put to use.** For example, if you simply walk from booth to booth at a trade show, tons of tools will be for sale to help your business, and there will be many similar

businesses you can learn from. If your business has slowed down, you have the time to do some research to help you get busy again!

4. **Always give as well as get.** Helping others can help you, too, as it did for me when I helped Chantel Ray. You never know when you're going to need advice or information or assistance, so don't be stingy when others come to you.

STEP 4

ACT:
YOU REAP WHAT YOU SOW,
100 PERCENT OF THE TIME

*"Patience, persistence, and perspiration make
an unbeatable combination for success."*
—Napoleon Hill

After working for two years at my first job, at
Grempler Realty, I went to work for Long & Foster, a
larger firm founded more than forty years ago that now
has 260 offices and over 17,000 sales associates. Based in
Fairfax, Virginia, Long & Foster is the largest privately
owned real estate company in the country and the largest

real estate company in the mid-Atlantic. That was the year my career really took off, and I more than tripled my income: In my second year in business, I earned $24,000 from my real estate commissions, but in my third year, I increased that to $83,000. And I was still only twenty-four years old!

My success at that time was because of the lessons I had learned from Floyd Wickman. I wanted to take my career—and my income—to the next level, so I had been looking for courses and seminars that would teach me a better way to work. I mentioned in Step 1 that I had attended one of Floyd's seminars, which he called "Sweat-hogs." He acted like a personal trainer who wanted to improve our business skills. During the seminar, the other attendees and I worked hard for several days to learn everything we could from him, and we would continue to implement his ideas for the next several months.

Floyd's course taught me that there was a way to go out and make things happen, instead of just waiting for business to come to me. Erv Norgren, the real estate agent who took me under his wing at Grempler Realty, was the first person to teach me to be proactive, but Floyd's course taught me how to do it at a much higher level. Many agents get into real estate thinking the leads are just going to come to them and that it's their job simply to *react* to leads, as if someone will throw a ball and it's their job simply to catch it. This is also true of many people in other industries, and not only salespeople but also many independent professionals, from freelance editors to electricians. If you want to succeed (or if you want to have *more* success *earlier* in your career), you need to be proactive and go out and find more customers.

Floyd's course taught me how important it is to show up every morning at 9:00 a.m., sit down at your desk, and call people until you get an appointment. That may sound simple—and it is—but it's a great way to get started on a successful career. I did exactly what Floyd recommended: I called all day long until I got an appointment. At first, it was tedious and frustrating, but that's the name of the game in sales (and if you're self-employed): It's a numbers game, so you have to make as many calls as you can in order to find prospective customers. You can't take rejection personally, and you can't let refusals get you down or distract you from picking up the phone and making another call.

There were days I averaged thirty calls an hour, which is 240 calls in an eight-hour day. Most of the calls were brief, because I got either an answering machine, no answer, or a busy signal, or I had very short conversations with the people I actually got through to. But I kept calling until I got an appointment with someone who was considering selling his or her house.

This was long before 2004, when the Do Not Call list went into effect and prevented this kind of random cold-calling; now, you have to make sure your prospects aren't listed there before you call. Nevertheless, I still do some cold-calling, as well as warm-calling to follow up on previous clients, and I've lately heard of more and more agents doing cold-calling with lists scrubbed of people on the Do Not Call list. It's one of the best ways I know to stay in touch and drum up business. To do warm-calling, all you need to do is call people you know in some capacity—and I'm sure you can come up with plenty if you think hard enough. If not, you can always join various organizations to meet more people—a place of worship, a volunteer organization, a hobby organization, etc. Anywhere you can meet new people opens up a whole new world of potential prospects. You just need to make warmer calls, rather than the cold calls of the past.

Of course, some of the most efficient calls to make are to expired listings or "for sale by owners." With both, you at least know you are calling someone who has already raised a hand and said, "I want to sell!"

STEP 4: ACT

Another lesson I learned about being proactive is to focus on "dollar-productive activities," which I mentioned briefly in Step 1. For example, as a real estate agent, you can do many different things during the course of a sales transaction. From the first time you meet someone who's interested in selling his or her home (or if you're meeting someone interested in buying a home) until the time you get to settlement, there are a lot of small tasks that need to be done. You need to deliver lockboxes, make copies of the contract, drop off a copy of the contract to the other agent involved in the sale, order a home inspection, meet with the various inspectors, etc. However, only certain activities and tasks actually make you money:

- prospecting for new sellers and buyers;
- meeting buyers and showing them homes (face-to-face with buyers);
- going on listing appointments (face-to-face with sellers);
- negotiating contracts.

These four activities actually make you money. In contrast, driving across town to deliver a contract to a client—which might take half an hour or more—is something you can *delegate* to somebody working for you, for $10 to $15 an hour. And I guarantee that no matter *what* business you're in, there are dollar-productive activities that only *you* can do, and then there's all the other work you need to do (or have someone else do) to support your business. So before you start doing all those non-dollar-productive tasks, figure out what your hourly rate of worth is. To get this rate, take your annual income and divide that by the number of hours you worked.

For example, suppose you earned $100,000 last year, and you worked a forty-hour week, with two weeks' vacation, so you worked fifty weeks: that's two thousand hours. When you divide $100,000 by two thousand hours, your hourly rate was $50 per hour. If you earned $250,000 and worked fifty hours each week with two weeks' vacation, your hourly rate was $100 per hour.

Next, calculate the time you spend on dollar-productive activities that require *your* attention—like the four activities I listed previously. You'll probably find that the total time you spend on these activities might be only five out of fifty hours a week.

If you can delegate the non-revenue-generating tasks you've been doing in the *other* forty-five hours each week, at a cost that is much less than your hourly rate, you'll find

DOLLAR-PRODUCTIVITY WORKSHEET

1. Yearly Income $ _____

2. Weekly Income $ _____ (#1 ÷ C)

3. Hourly Income $ _____ (#2 ÷ A)

4. Dollar-Productive Hourly Income $ _____ (#2 ÷ B)

A = # of hours I work weekly   _____

B = # of hours I prospect, list,
     work w/ buyers & negotiate   _____

C = # of weeks I work in a year
     (52 total) (subtract vacations)   _____

that your time is worth much more. Assume you make $250,000 a year, work fifty weeks a year, but are spending only five hours a week on dollar-productive work: Your dollar-productive hourly income is $1,000. When you focus on doing only the revenue-producing activities and delegating all the non-revenue-producing activities, then you're going to make so much *more* money! (Or you'll have forty-five extra hours of free time!)

Unfortunately, many real estate agents, small business owners, and independent professionals often do everything themselves. In real estate, 90 percent of an agent's time is spent on doing paperwork and delivering it to clients—again, work that's largely administrative. But if you look at a transaction like the sale of a home, which basically starts with meeting buyers, putting them in your car, showing them houses, writing an offer, and negotiating the offer with the other agent—those activities are dollar-productive. The more of those you do, the more money you make.

In other words, you either *have* an assistant or you *are* an assistant. In real estate, if you're taking pictures of a house, you're acting as the photographer, not a real estate agent, so you have to figure that time as what a photographer should be paid. But if you count up the hours you spend each year on your dollar-productive activities, you might be worth thousands of dollars an hour. In contrast, when you spend your time making copies, you're the assistant, and that time is worth only an assistant's hourly rate.

In light of this, you should pay someone else to take pictures, make copies of sell sheets, and perform other administrative tasks. Your goal should be to do more dollar-productive activities.

Here are three great ways to figure out what your non–dollar-productive activities are:

STEP 4: ACT

1. Take a day to stay at home and delegate to someone else (e.g., an assistant, if you have one). Give this person anything that you would normally do, as you would if you were on vacation or sick in the hospital. By doing that, you'll find that your assistant is so much more capable than you thought, and that he or she can do a lot of the tasks you typically do. Many people simply need an opportunity to rise to the occasion, and you have to give them that opportunity. Then, while you're home, focus on the really productive work—such as calling past clients or calling vendors you work with and asking them who they know who needs to buy or sell a house.

2. Write down your activities every fifteen minutes. Get an egg timer, set it for fifteen minutes, and when it goes off, write down what you did. At the end of the day, you'll see immediately how much time you wasted: you'll realize you were on Facebook, or sending e-mails, or talking to friends about nonwork activities—none of which have helped you make any money. These are the activities you need to cut out.

3. Turn off your cell phone and don't answer your e-mail until noon. This enables you to work at least from 9:00 a.m. to 12:00 p.m. doing things that are critically important to your business, whatever they are in your work. In Step 1 I mentioned the book *Never Check E-Mail in the Morning*—which is good advice! Don't get distracted by what other people want from you; instead, *you* should decide what work is most important, and do that first.

After learning these lessons from Dr. Fred Grosse's course, as soon as I got back to my office, I hired more assistants. I also started my own personal accountability program when I started e-mailing David Osborn (the peer partner I mentioned in Step 1). Every day, I e-mailed him the number of hours I had worked and how many of those hours were spent on dollar-productive activities.

In my case, I want to have twenty hours of dollar-productivity every week. Most people are "at work" for an entire day, but when they look back on what they've actually done, in terms of making real money, they find they actually did only half an hour of productive work and seven and a half hours of crap work. Personally, I don't want to waste my time doing non–dollar-productive work when I can delegate that to others (and I'll provide more information on delegating in Step 5).

Finally, if you don't have anything to do, don't just

sit around! Instead, call dead leads, the people who were interested a few years ago but never bought. It has worked for me, and it can work for you, too!

––––––

During my first couple of years in business, I learned not only that I had to make my own success by cold-calling persistently and following up consistently; I also learned that *when the phone rings, there's money to be made.* I've seen lots of agents just waiting for the phone to ring so that they could get new business. (Remember the gregarious, big-haired women I worked with at my first job? That's what they did all day long.) Even worse, when the phone *does* ring, I've seen lots of agents squander leads because they felt those leads weren't "good enough."

I'm sure you've seen this, too. In every industry, there are people who wait for business to come to them, and then there are people who continually go out and find new customers.

The office manager at Grempler Realty, a guy named George Holman, had worked for Grempler for twenty-five years; he had started as an agent, like me, and he had sold thousands of homes successfully for the first twenty years of his career. Finally the owner promoted him to manager of one of the offices, with thirty other agents to manage. George was a short, skinny guy in his mid-forties, with red hair and a mustache and beard, and he talked all the time; if you asked him a question, he went on and on and on. George was a true salesman at heart. He could have sold ice to Eskimos, and he had been a phenomenal agent. Eventually he moved to a different role in the company, but because George had been an agent, he got frustrated at times when he felt that the agents in the office weren't working hard enough.

So one day, George sat everybody down at an office meeting and he said, "This company lost $34,000 yesterday." Every person there was stunned and wanted to know what the heck George could possibly be talking about. So he explained: "We got seven calls from ads we ran, from people who called in to ask for more information on these properties. But did we sell anything? No. Did we even *show* anything? No. And when I asked some of you why none of these calls panned out, here's what several of you told me:

- The first caller 'just didn't seem like a serious buyer.'

- The second caller 'didn't seem to be qualified to get a mortgage.'

- The third caller 'acted like she was already working with another real estate agent, so she didn't want to work with us.'

- The fourth caller 'just started looking, so he probably isn't really ready to buy anything yet.'

- The fifth caller 'was "just curious."'

- The sixth caller 'was just a nosy neighbor.'

- The seventh caller 'said, "I'm looking for a friend."'

"In reality, all seven of these people are going to buy or sell a house, and these reasons that we should not work with them are all just excuses." And he explained how:

- "Caller #1 might not be a serious buyer *right now*, but that person was interested enough to call us to find out more about one of our properties. So if the agent who had taken that call had taken the time to show Caller #1 that property (and others similar to it, or in the same price range), that agent could have made a sale. Maybe not that day, but maybe eventually, when that buyer finally did decide he was ready to buy.

- "Similarly, Caller #2 may not have 'seemed' to be qualified to get a mortgage, but until the agent knew that for sure, the agent who took her call should have worked with her further. Again, it's a lead, and leads are *valuable*!

- "Caller #3 may have already been working with a buyer agent, so it's true that the agent who took her call wouldn't get paid, but if the call had been handled more assertively, we might have been able to get the name of the buyer's agent and give it to the listing agent, so at least the office would potentially get a listing commission out of the deal. In that case, you would be acting as a secretary, but you're still helping your co-workers and your company as a whole by doing a favor for the listing agent.

- "Just because Caller #4 just started looking doesn't mean he's not going to buy one of the first houses he sees. Some buyers just know what they want and buy the first or second house they see; never assume everyone wants to look at dozens of houses.

- "Caller #5 may indeed have been 'just curious,' but curiosity is often the beginning of an actual house search. It doesn't necessarily mean it's a dead lead.

- "Similarly, Caller #6 may have been a nosy neighbor, but usually people are nosy for a reason. They may be thinking of selling their house, so they want to know what a house is selling for so they can value their own house.

- "Finally, if Caller #7 was calling for a friend, you should have asked if we can call that friend directly."

What George showed us that day was that the agents who rejected those calls as not worth pursuing had done so because they had put their own mental spin on each call; these agents had prejudged the callers, because of either their tone of voice or something they said. And this happens frequently in real estate sales.

I was guilty of it myself very early in my career. I took a call from a guy, and because of the way he talked, I thought he was mentally disabled. But because my mama raised me to be a nice person, I was polite to him and answered his questions. He was calling about a townhouse that cost about $80,000 (and this was in 1990). He asked me how much it cost, what the square footage was, what the condition of the property was, and anything else I could tell him that wasn't covered in the listing.

I gave him all the information he requested. But just like the agents George described that day at Grempler, I didn't really think he was a serious buyer, so I was just about to blow him off and hang up when I decided to ask him one question of my own: "How long have you been looking?" And that's when he told me, "Well, I'm not looking for myself; I'm looking to buy a property for my gardener."

"What?" I asked.

I couldn't believe what I had heard, because I had a preconception in my mind about this caller, simply because he spoke so slowly and seemed to have difficulty even articulating his simple questions. But my caller repeated what he was looking for: "I've got this guy who works for me, mending the fences on my property, and his wife is a maid in our house. They're getting ready to have a baby, so the living quarters we have for them aren't big enough anymore, so I've decided to buy him a townhouse to live in."

Of course, I continued to talk to him, asking more about the type of property he was interested in buying for his gardener and housekeeper, and by the end of our conversation, I found out that my caller was one of the richest men in the state of Maryland, and that he owned dozens of properties and hundreds of acres of farmland already (which is why he employed someone just to repair his fences). Everyone in my office knew who he was except me! I sold him a three-bedroom, two-and-a-half-bath townhouse, which was perfect for the gardener, his wife, and their soon-to-be baby. That house cost around $125,000, so I made about $2,000 in commission.

I'll never forget that day. I had prejudged this caller by his voice alone, and I had decided he couldn't possibly be a serious buyer. I was lucky I was polite to him and answered his questions—and that I asked one question that happened to reveal who my caller was. This was the exact same point George Holman made the day he ran through all the excuses he had heard about why all the incoming calls weren't viable or valuable leads.

There was one agent in particular—I'll call him Henry Clark—who completely prejudged everybody who called him, and therefore never followed up on those calls. Henry was a good person: He was an older gentleman who had retired from full-time work but was still working with us. He showed up every day, he was always in the office, he was reliable, and he answered the phones. But Henry didn't really sell any houses, because he didn't really follow up on the calls he took, and he prejudged the potential customers who called. He had a negative thing to say about every single prospect.

George wanted Henry and all of us agents to see

that every call has a dollar sign attached to it. As George said, "You need to realize that when that phone rings, if someone's asking you how much a house is, that call is potentially worth at least a couple of thousand dollars in commission. Think of your phone as a money phone: You should see dollar signs and hear a *ka-ching* every time it rings. And when you answer the phone, handle it like an egg. Don't blow off any call, because you can so easily lose thousands of dollars if you blow it."

Okay, so George mixed his metaphors (the phone was a cash register, and the phone was an egg). Big deal. He may not have been the most eloquent speaker, but he taught me a great lesson, which I've passed on to every person who has ever worked for me. I'll pass it on here, too: *Every single call is valuable, and every single lead is valuable.*

This is true no matter what business you're in or what type of work you do. Figure out what your average commission is, and every time the phone rings, that's the dollar value you should have in mind.

Most people don't realize that. The reality is that for a real estate agent—or anyone working in sales—nothing is more important than meeting clients. In order to meet clients, you have to make phone calls. If you have eight

BUYER LEAD SHEET

Date _____

Agent assigned to the lead _____ Call accepted by (Team Member) _____

Name _____

Phone _____

Email _____

What is the address of the home you are inquiring about? _____

What prompted you to call? _____

Are you working with a REALTOR®? _____ How long? _____ If so, have you signed an agreement? _____

Are you looking to Purchase or Rent a home? _____

Can you tell me about the home you are searching for?

Price Range _____ Desired Cities _____ Schools _____

Condo _____ Townhome _____ Single Family _____

Bedrooms _____ # Baths _____ Basement _____ Garage _____ Fireplace _____

Will you be paying cash or will you be financing the home? _____

Have you been pre-approved by a lender? _____ Who did you speak with? _____

Mortgage Information

Appointment set for _____ When were you prequalified? _____

Mortgage Company _____ Sales price _____

Loan Officer _____ Type of loan _____

Phone _____ Rates and terms _____

If NOT prequalified please schedule a time when a loan officer can call them.

Do you currently (circle one)   Own   or   Rent

If own, do you need to sell your home to make your next purchase? _____

If your home is not yet on the market, would you like to have a market analysis done on your current home to determine its current value? _____

If you rent, when does your lease expire? _____

What date and time are you available to see the home(s)? _____

Find them on:

Facebook _____   LinkedIn _____

Twitter _____   Did you Google them? _____

We have copies of this form in the office for when buyers call in. Once a week the buyers' agents bring us their lead sheets from the prior week and we discuss them. Some agents will then enter leads into a follow-up database. Others simply have a file for every month, and if they need to follow up with the prospect in an upcoming month—say, February—they will drop the form into the February folder and pull it out on February 1.

hours in a day and spend half an hour meeting clients, that's your most important half hour. The other seven and a half hours don't matter. If all you did all day were meet with clients, you would make more money than an agent who worked seven and a half hours in the office but didn't meet a single client. The same applies to prospect calls: If you get only one call a day from a prospect, that's probably the most important call you'll get, and you should treat it that way.

In addition to being persistent and efficient with their time, successful businesspeople don't get complacent. It's great if you're getting business just by word of mouth and referrals from past clients, but you also need to proactively continue to market your business.

That marketing doesn't necessarily need to be sophisticated advertising—especially if you're satisfied with the level and volume of business you're doing and the profit you're earning. But you should continue to put yourself out there and make others aware that you're always interested in new business. If you don't, your business could dry up faster than an indoor plant you forget to water.

Marketing yourself can often be as simple as asking

someone for his or her business. For example, I ran into one of my neighbors at the gym—let's call him Bob— and while we were running next to each other on the treadmills, Bob told me he had listed his house with one of my competitors because that competitor had told him I had just laid off six people, so he thought my business was in trouble. I realize that just because someone lives in my neighborhood doesn't mean they'll hire me when they decide to sell their house, but this particular story bothered me. Bob thought we weren't doing well and therefore weren't up to the job. He said he felt bad about hiring someone else instead of me, but still, that's what he'd done.

I went back to the office that day and I shared this story with some of my team, but I kept thinking about it even after talking to them. Clearly, it was bugging me. So a couple of days later, when I saw Bob at the gym again, I went up to him and said, "Hey, Bob, I've been thinking about what you said the other day, about how you felt bad about hiring another agent instead of me. I know your parents are going to sell their house. Can I sell it for them?" I didn't say anything else; I just waited for him to respond. Sure enough, he said, "Yeah, I guess I owe that to you. I'll let you sell their house when the time comes."

So I got a verbal commitment from him. I knew his parents weren't going to put their house on the market until after he sold his, because he was planning to move to Virginia Beach, and his parents were going to move into a retirement home near his new house. But I left that thought in his mind: He had made me a promise that he would hire me to sell his parents' house. Essentially, I had simply asked him point-blank whether I could have his business. Because we were neighbors, and because he felt bad about letting someone else sell his home, he was happy to let me sell his parents' property.

Many other businesspeople would have just brushed off Bob's comment at the gym and written off the sale of his house as lost business. But I decided simply to ask him straight out if he would give me a chance to show him what I can do.

My point is that you need to continue to ask for new business, even if you've been in business for years or even decades. *If you don't ask, you probably won't get the work.*

Also, many people might think that a promise isn't worth much; they think that someone *saying* they'll do something doesn't mean they really *will* when the time comes. But contrary to popular belief, 80 percent of the people who give you their word will not only remember that they did so, but also honor that promise. So when Bob gave me his word that he would hire me to sell his parents' house, that not only alleviated his guilt, it also helped reopen the door to our business relationship. In other words, if I hadn't asked him for his business, he might have been too embarrassed or too worried that I was angry with him to ever call me again and *offer* his business.

And sure enough, that's exactly what happened. Unfortunately for Bob, the agent he had hired wasn't able to sell his house. So a few months later, Bob called me and said, "My home is still on the market, and I'm ready to make a change." He asked me if I was interested in taking a crack at selling his house. I said, "Absolutely, I'd love your business." So I ended up selling not only his parents' house, but his as well.

In this case, I started with nothing and ended up with two deals. Not bad for asking one simple question! Now think about whose business *you* can ask for.

———

As I've just shown, sometimes you need to remind your clients of the commitments they've made. If you do it gently, it can work to your advantage and theirs. Here's another example.

A guy who worked in our office building—let's call him Tom—used to come in to our office often to ask for information on the real estate market. Tom let us know he had a fairly large house, and he promised us he wasn't just pumping us and working with another real estate company. Whenever he asked us questions about the real estate market, he always said things like, "Listen, I'm not wasting your time. When I list my house, I'm going to list it with you."

I didn't mind talking to Tom from time to time and giving him updates on the market and various neighborhoods. This went on for several years. But when it came time to list his house, he told me, "You know, you don't do a lot of business in my area. I'm thinking about using another real estate agent who's very prominent in our neighborhood. In fact, I've already had him out to the house and I'm thinking of moving forward with him."

This is a situation real estate professionals face all the time, and many people think that the right thing to do is just be gracious and let the client do whatever he wants to do. Many businesspeople think that by the time the client has already contacted someone else, the game is over, and there's no salvaging this deal.

But the game isn't over until the contract is signed.

So in this case, I said to him, "Tom, I understand what you're thinking, but there's one reason why you should list your house with me." And he said, "Okay, what is it?" I told him, "Because you told me you would." And that's all I said.

Tom was surprised, and he stammered a bit. But finally he admitted, "You're right, I did tell you that." Then I went a little further and said, "My grandfather always told me, a man's only as good as his word. I'll leave it up to you, but that's why you should list your house with me."

So Tom listed his house with my company. And we sold it.

Many people think that because their words are not in writing or in print that I can't hold them to what they've said in conversation. But if you give your commitment, the only way you can get out of it is if I *let* you out of it. Also, many businesspeople are reluctant even to ask for a commitment, but one of the questions we ask often is simply, "Can I be your agent?" You may not want to be that direct, but it's really a great way to get business.

The point is, if you remind people that they've given you their word, they won't want to be liars, and they'll honor their word. All you need to do is ask them straight out, put it out there, and let them give you a commitment.

It doesn't matter if it's not in writing. Admittedly, every once in a while you'll find someone who goes back on his or her commitment, but that's pretty rare. In general, nine out of ten people will stick to their word, especially if you remind them of it.

In Step 3, I described how I followed up with clients months after our last contact, and I recommend the same here: If someone tells you they're thinking of buying or selling or working with you in six months, or if someone tells you, "We just need to wait until the spring," or "We need to sell our vacation home in Hawaii first," don't assume that means they're not interested in working with you. Instead, ask them the next question: "If you list your house, or when you list it, will you list it with me?" Then just let them answer.

Of course, they might tell you no, or they might leave things open-ended, saying something like, "I don't know, I'd like to interview more agents." But if you ask people directly for their business, you're at least giving them an opportunity to say yes, and if they say yes, all you need to do is tell them, "Great, I look forward to working with you." You're so much further ahead with that verbal commitment than you are with no commitment at all. Too many people think it's not worth anything unless it's in writing, so they think they might as well not even ask. Don't think that way. Go ahead and ask!

Finally, many people have asked me how they can be successful even when their business is in a slump. That happens to every business from time to time, but especially when your entire industry or the economy as a whole is suffering. The first time it happened to me was when I left Long & Foster and went to work at RE/MAX. The owner of RE/MAX had pumped me up so much in front of the other people working there that I felt like a big shot coming in. Because of that, and because I took the biggest office available and had a massive desk, everyone in the office expected a lot of me. Then I fell flat on my face. I didn't sell anything at all during the first few months I worked there. And I remember sitting in my big office with my big desk and feeling humiliated that every agent in the office was slapping sales up on the sales board while my name was nowhere to be seen.

I was in a slump, which happens to everyone on occasion. Fortunately, I realized I had fallen victim to a trap that many real estate agents fall into: We sometimes lose track of what's really important in business—which is how much money we're actually netting on the bottom line. In fact, research studies and surveys have found that some people—especially salespeople—work harder for *recognition* than they do for money. Real estate salespeople in particular love to see their names up on a sales board as being "the number-one seller for the month [or year]." But that's not what's really important; what really matters is how much money you're making for yourself and your business. So over the course of my career, I've developed what I call "twelve ways to get out of a slump," as described in the box that follows.

TWELVE WAYS TO GET OUT OF A SLUMP

1. Be proactive, not reactive. Successful people are productive every morning. In sales, that means you need to be making prospecting calls, doing open houses, calling clients (past, present, and future), writing notes to people, making new contacts, and getting in people's faces. Don't just sit around and wait for the phone to ring—go out and get some business!

2. Get back to the basics. Call anyone who is a potential target. In my business, I call FSBOs (short for "for sale

---

by owner") to see if they might consider hiring an agent instead of trying to sell their houses themselves. And I call listings that another agent had but that have expired to see if that seller might be interested in hiring me to try to sell his or her house. Whatever your business is, you need to get back to your dollar-productive activities.

3. Don't turn down any business. If you're not busy and someone comes to you with a small job, take it anyway, because it may lead to a larger job later on. For example, we occasionally get calls from people who are looking to rent something for, say, only $600 a month. Obviously, we make only $100 in commission on that type of work. But if we're not busy, we'll do it. Say yes to that business just so you'll be active and get your blood flowing again. A lot of people don't do that because they don't want to "waste" their time doing small projects while they're waiting for the one big project or the one big client. Don't do that. Don't just sit at home or in your office. Do *something*, even if it's small!

4. Write thank-you notes. You should write these to everyone: past clients, vendors you've worked with, anyone who has helped you in the past, anyone you meet or can get an address for. Go crazy. Send a note to anyone you can think of. Put your name in front of people so they'll think of you when they're ready to buy or sell real estate.

5. Get busy. In my business, we often list a property even when we think it's not going to sell. We list it just to keep us busy and to generate buyer calls from the sign. Activity breeds activity, and one thing often leads to another. Find *something* you can do to keep yourself busy and working; don't just sit around waiting for the phone to ring. Every client interaction should build subtle self-confidence in you.

6. Plan out your week. Even if you don't have appointments with potential clients, make appointments with someone you know, from whom you could ask for referrals. That way you'll get out of the office, see people, take meetings, and again, keep busy.

7. Accept all invitations. When they're busy, many people turn down invitations. They don't need new business, so they focus on the business they have and the leisure and family activities they want to enjoy when they're not working. But when you're *not* working or you're in a slump, you should accept every invitation you get, so you can network and pass out as many business cards as you can. A lot of people don't want to do this because they don't want to admit they're not busy at work, but that's exactly why you *should* get out and network and meet new people—or even old friends who may know someone who's looking for just the service you're providing. When you're in a slump, you need to become a social butterfly. Create a massive social calendar.

8. Don't panic. Keep in mind the tightrope theory: *Don't look down.* Move forward, and stay active. If you're looking down, if you seem depressed, customers will notice. Just keep going.

9. Look successful. Even when the going gets rough, you need to continue to go to your office or workplace looking sharp. You need to look good so you'll feel good—trust me, it works! Even if you don't have any appointments, just being dressed up in a suit will get you going and keep you going.

10. Stay away from negative people and negativity in general. Ignore the naysayers, even if it's the daily newspaper proclaiming that the market or economy is down. You need to stay positive.

11. Motivate yourself. Go to as many motivational seminars as you can, listen to motivational downloads, read motivational books—basically, you want to inject as much positivity into yourself as you can to get your mind out of a slump. You can learn new ways to get business at these seminars, and even if you pick up just one new idea, that's worth it. Plus, again, by getting out of your workplace, you'll meet people, and you never know what those connections will lead you to.

12. Volunteer. In my business, I recommend offering to host other people's open houses, or volunteering to answer the phone in case a lead comes in. When you feel a slump coming on, volunteer to help someone else in your business, company, or industry until your own business picks up. Don't give in to an attitude that some types of work are beneath you.

YOUR 7-FIGURE GAME PLAN

1. **Don't sit around waiting for business to come to you—be proactive!** The more people you call, the more sales you are likely to make. Go out and find them.

2. **Spend as much of your time as possible on dollar-productive activities that only you can do.** Don't waste your valuable time doing paperwork or other tasks that someone else could easily handle. Remember, you either *have* an assistant or you *are* an assistant!

3. **Don't squander leads.** Keep in mind that every time the phone rings or someone walks through the door, that's potential business. Treat everyone as though they are *already* customers. You'll be surprised at how much more business you get!

4. **Continue to market your business; don't get complacent.** Even if business is good—even if it's great—you should continue to promote your company. That doesn't mean you need to spend a ton of money on advertising or other expensive marketing methods, but you do need to ensure that past, present, and future customers know that you're always interested in doing business with them.

5. **Get verbal commitments from prospective customers.** You don't always need a written contract—although if you can get that, it's great to have. But

in the early stages of developing a relationship with prospective clients or customers, it may be inappropriate to ask them to sign a contract. It's not inappropriate at all to ask them for their word that they will work with you if they decide they need or want what you're offering. Fortunately, most people honor their word and will give you that business when they're ready.

6. **Don't get stuck in a slump.** Every business has its ups and downs, especially when the economy falters. Review the list that starts on page 120 whenever you feel stuck. If my business could survive the real estate meltdown that began in 2007, your business can survive, too!

STEP 5

BUILD ON IT!
CAPITALIZE ON EVERY SUCCESS,
NO MATTER HOW SMALL

*"I am convinced that nothing we do is more important
than hiring and developing people. At the end of the day,
you bet on people, not strategies."*
—Larry Bossidy, retired CEO of AlliedSignal and
former vice chairman of General Electric

In Step 3, I mentioned that one of the very first lessons I learned from my first mentor, Erv Norgren, was to be proactive. That's how I started to be successful in business: I didn't just sit around waiting for potential customers to call me; instead, I went out and found them. That same trait has helped me build and grow my business by leveraging every successful sale I made—and even every contact I made. Back in my cold-calling days, if the people I called had no interest in selling their homes, I didn't end the conversation there; I asked the next sensible question, which might lead me to a prospect: "Do you know anyone else who might be thinking of selling his or her house?"

It's a simple question, but I've heard way too many salespeople hang up the phone after they get the first no. (Remember the seven excuses described in Step 4?) In other words, don't take no for an answer, even if the person you're talking to has no interest in buying or selling property; before that person slips away, you should at least leverage the contact by asking for another lead.

I've always asked the question I learned in my cold-calling days before hanging up or walking away from a potential deal. It led me to my first cold-call sale, for a client named John Olson. I had called his next-door neighbor and asked my usual question: "Have you thought about selling your house?" She said no. But I followed up by asking her, "Well, who do you know who needs to buy or sell a home in the next six months?" She said, "Well, the house next door has been empty for about a year and a half. I think the owner has wanted to sell it for a long time, but it needs a lot of work." I asked her what the owner's name was. She told me it was John Olson, and I decided to try to find him.

I tracked him down through the phone book. I had to call a few John Olsons before I found the right one, but that's part of the numbers game, too, and I figured that eventually, I would find the guy I was looking for. Sure enough, I got ahold of him. He was living in an apartment, and I persuaded him to meet me at the house he wanted to sell. He told me he wanted to fix it up but he just hadn't gotten around to it, which happens often when people want to sell a property; they simply find the project overwhelming.

Frankly, I could see why renovating this house would be overwhelming to John. The weeds were extremely high. The deck in the back was falling off; it was dangerous to go out on it because the wood was so rotted. It was a three-bedroom house that had been built in 1930, and it looked like nothing had been done to it since then: The tile in the bathroom was apple green (a popular color in the 1930s and '40s), and there was only one bathroom, not even a powder room on the first floor. The kitchen cabinets were metal and painted white, which probably looked great in a farmhouse during the Depression, but it just didn't work sixty years later. Finally, the hardwood floors in the bedrooms had probably been beautiful once, but they were worn down almost beyond repair, and most buyers in the late 1980s wanted wall-to-wall carpeting anyway. Even the electricity needed to be updated: There were no overhead fixtures in any of the rooms, since that wasn't the style of lighting in the 1930s. John didn't want to renovate the house himself, and he couldn't afford to hire a team to do it for him, which is what he would have needed to do in order to sell it for a higher price.

So I asked John, "What price would you sell it for, as is?" He named his price, which was quite low; we put it on the market, and it sold right away. John had wanted to sell this house for a year and a half, but he hadn't done anything about it. I got the listing—and I made the sale— simply because I was persistent and consistent about call- ing people. I had cold-called his next-door neighbor, I had tracked down the right John Olson, and then I called him and persuaded him to put his house on the market, as is, and get whatever he could for it. John was able to realize his primary goal, which was to sell that house, and he was delighted that I had gotten that property off his hands. In fact, he was so grateful that when I asked him to write me a testimonial, he gave me a truly lavish endorsement:

> It was my good fortune and great pleasure to have Pat handle the sale of my home in Centennial Estates. Thanks to Pat's professionalism, patience, persistence, and thoroughness, the property sold so quickly I was amazed. I could not be more pleased with Pat's performance.
>
> —John L. Olson, Ellicott City, Maryland

Then I did everything I could to leverage that sale to find new clients. A typical agent probably would have called a hundred people who lived near that house to see if they also were interested in selling their properties. But I called about *two thousand* people. Literally. I called people who lived even three or four miles away and said, "I'm Pat Hiban, I just sold a house on Century Drive, and I'm calling to see if you'd thought about selling your house now or in the near future." Some people realized the house I had sold wasn't really in their neighborhood, but most people didn't even ask: They just assumed it was a house near them. And they assumed I was an expert on their neighborhood—why else would I be calling?

You need to do the same thing in your business: Whenever you get a new account, or increase your business, or achieve any success you can leverage, you need to spread the word to other potential customers. Contact other people or businesses nearby; people are always more willing to do business with someone who has already worked successfully in their general vicinity. Build your business by building on your successes, no matter how small.

———

Just as I was persistent when I first started to build my career, I was also persistent about growing my business even when the economy was suffering. I realized I needed to break into the foreclosure business, because that was what was selling best during that time. At first, I was very reluctant to try selling this type of property, because the word on the street was that the banks were "locked up" and not accepting new agents at this time. If you weren't in already, you'd never get in. But as the real estate market continued to decline and the number of foreclosures and short sales continued to increase, I realized I needed to get into foreclosures, no matter how difficult it was to break through. I needed to make sure my business was going where the money was flowing (as I discussed in Step 2).

STEP 5: BUILD ON IT!

Because my experience with foreclosures was extremely limited, I had to use what limited experience I had and build on it. Fifteen years prior, I had sold two homes for a local bank that had since gone out of business. Luckily, I had kept in touch with a loan officer from that bank, who was still working in the banking business. I called him and asked him to be a reference. He was happy to help, and I began to build on my fifteen-year-old success by letting banks know I did have Real Estate Owned (REO) experience.

I soon landed a small local bank that gave me one listing for $29,000. The property was a two-bedroom, single-family bungalow located in Maryland, very close to the DC border. It was a detached house, not a row home, but it was very small. There were only ten houses on this street, and seven of them were vacant and boarded up, so it was clearly a very poor location. The house had been on the market with another agent who had listed it for $186,000 because the previous owner had spent $150,000 on it. (I'm guessing he bought it for $100,000 and then put $50,000 worth of repairs and renovation into it). That owner was probably hoping to flip it, but then the bottom dropped out of the real estate market, and he was stuck with it. Interestingly, the bank tried to *give* this property to Habitat for Humanity, but the organization turned it down. It was clearly a tough sell, and it took us about eight months to find a buyer, but we finally sold it to an investor for $18,000.

I then built on that sale. I asked the new bank if it had listings with other agents. It did, and I got the bank's permission to advertise them for free, even though they were not my listings. I created an ad with all the bank's foreclosures and my picture, using it as proof that I was the foreclosure agent of choice. This helped me get in with others. For each new bank I got, I listed it on my e-mail signature and on my cards:

15 years' experience in REOs.

REO Clients:

Bay National Bank

American Home Funding

Bank of America

And so on. I soon built my new foreclosures business to more than thirty banks, all giving me listings simultaneously. Today I have forty-one. I believe my agency is now the number-one REO team in Maryland, with more than 320 foreclosures for sale. So even when the real estate market was down, we found a way to build our business by learning how to sell new types of property.

For every major endeavor I take on, I journal intensely about it first. I create the blueprints of how I am going to go about reaching the goal. The same way a builder needs architectural drawings, we need to map out how we plan to build our businesses.

My journals of the last 20 years.

In 2005, I decided that I needed to get into the luxury home market. Even though I had sold over five hundred homes the year prior, not a single one was over a million dollars. In fact, I realized I hadn't sold a home at that price in the past twelve years. I set a goal to sell ten homes worth over a million dollars in 2006. Then I went to work in my journal, mapping out how I was going to do that by building on one success after the other.

The first thing I needed to do was get my first listing in that price range. To me it was more important to have it than to sell it because I was using it solely as a building block. I instantly sat down and started calling the expired listings of any home over $1 million. Soon enough we listed a house in that range. It was a $1.2 million listing with a tax assessment of $650,000, so it was grossly overpriced. I knew it would never sell, but I printed fifty brochures of it, posted it prominently on my website, and bought the front page of the homes magazine for it.

Soon enough we received a listing call from someone who saw it on the front of the magazine and had a $1.4 million home to sell. We brought several copies of our $1.2 million brochure and spread them out on the table in front of the seller, showing him the type of marketing we do and giving him social proof that we specialize in that price range. He listed with us, and soon we had two listings over a million. Again we built on that success. The expired listing soon took the house off the market because not a single buyer looked at it. I didn't throw away all of our marketing on it, though. I had fifty beautiful brochures of it that I continued to use as examples. I left it on our website through the entire year.

Soon, we listed a $2.4 million house and sold it very quickly. Using my building plan, we took fifty brochures from that home and hung them on every doorknob in the neighborhood. The brochures said, "This is the type of marketing we used to sell your neighbor's house; we will use this to sell yours too." Thirty days after that, we listed the home next door to the original property for $2.1 million. That sold in a few months too. Every success became the building block for the next success, and by the end of the year, we had settled exactly ten homes at more than $1 million.

What is a success that you have had that you could build on?

———

Another way to "build on it" and grow your business is to leverage yourself through a team. After all, there's only so much time in a day. If you tried to build a home by yourself, it would take a decade, but if you have a team of contractors help you, it could get done in months. In every business, you reach a point where you can't do everything yourself, and where you really need to hire help. If you're doing a good job, people will refer you more and more business, and you obviously want to accept those referrals. It would be unnatural to decline by saying, "No, I can't take on any more business—I want to work only forty hours per week, and right now I'm already working forty-two hours." You might turn down smaller projects or smaller sales because you're not going to make as much commission, but no one's going to turn down what could be a $5,000 commission on the sale of a house.

Instead, most people accept referrals for new business and start working fifty hours a week. Then, when they get even *more* referrals, they accept those too and end up working sixty hours a week, seventy hours a week, and so on. For most real estate agents, small businesses, and independent professionals, it's virtually unheard of to turn down qualified business opportunities: People who work for themselves typically just work longer hours and keep adding to their workweek.

Because of that tendency, it's important to learn how

to hire good people to help you with some of your work—and then delegate appropriate activities to your staff. Unfortunately, many people struggle with delegation, which is one reason I teach a class on the subject. Building a great team is essential to the success of a growing business.

Interestingly, though, most real estate agents are solo practitioners: They tend to work independently, and they don't hire a staff or a team to help them with their workload or grow their business. In fact, according to a NATIONAL ASSOCIATION of REALTORS® member profile that surveyed its 1.3 million REALTOR® members (which is about half of all real estate licensees in the United States), only one in five REALTORS®—20 percent—has at least one personal assistant. And there's no statistical information on how many of that 20 percent have a larger staff or team.

Of course, many people who become real estate agents *want* to work alone: To them, that's the appeal of that type of work. But you can't grow if you're doing everything yourself. In many cases, though, you can hire people to do some of the jobs that you're doing yourself, and your staff can do those tasks at a much cheaper cost, thereby allowing you to earn more!

My success in team-building comes mostly from hiring good, solid, talented team members. In fact, I believe the biggest challenge many businesspeople have is hiring good people and building a team. Once you're successful as a solo entrepreneur—in any business—there's a natural tendency to want to grow even more and do an even higher volume of business. Since there's only so much you can do yourself, the only way to grow your business is, obviously, to add people who can help you. Remember the dollar-productive activities I mentioned in Steps 1 and 4. You want to focus on those, and hire people to handle everything else.

I hired my first lasting staff member after I had been in business for about eight years. I worked completely solo for my first five years in business, then I had a partner, and after a year and a half or so we hired an assistant to help both of us. My partner and I had different ideas on how to grow the business, so we dissolved our partnership amicably and let that assistant go. I worked on my own for the next six months, until I realized I needed someone to work as my right-hand man (or woman) as an executive assistant. I hired someone I knew already: Greg was a receptionist for RE/MAX. I thought we would work well together, and we did. I delegated all my administrative tasks to him: He handled all my calls and all the inputting of information into our client database (to keep track of potential, current, and past clients) and all processing and follow-up. Anything he couldn't handle, he turned over to me. It was great: We had a strong bond and a solid working relationship, and he worked for me for almost two years.

Later in the year that I hired Greg, I hired my first buyer agent, someone who would work exclusively with buyers (so I could focus on sellers). Her name was Janice Mattson, and she's still with me today, fifteen years later. I found Janice by putting the word out that I was looking to add a buyer agent to my team, but no one had ever heard of this concept before. I had learned it at a seminar from another agent who told me he was hiring an agent to work exclusively with buyers, and that made a lot of sense to me, given that listings are so important.

After all, when a seller hires you to sell his or her property, you have something tangible to work with: You have a product—someone's home—and all you need to do is find the right buyer. Not that finding the right buyer is easy, but you can control your listing appointments, whereas it's harder to control buyers. If you have to prioritize your time between buyers and sellers, buyers are secondary. While you can't be sure a buyer will buy something, sellers are (for the most part) definitely motivated to sell their homes. Moreover, buyers can easily take up a whole weekend: They want to see properties, typically lots of properties, and they want you to show them right away. If you don't, they're going to work with somebody else.

In contrast, a seller typically calls and says, "I'd like to talk to you about selling my house." Then, you make an appointment for a time that works for both you and the seller; there's no real set time that you *have* to go. In other words, you have control over your schedule, though of course you want to accommodate your client as much as you can. A listing appointment is only a two- or three-hour job, and once you have the listing, most of the work for the seller is done in the office during regular business hours, Monday through Friday, 9:00 to 5:00.

With buyers, you typically don't have that option. If you want to sell them something, you need to be at their beck and call and work according to their schedule, and they often will want to go out on weekends and evenings, maybe for months, before they make a decision to buy a property. You can spend forty hours with a buyer, showing dozens of properties, and *still* not sell a house!

Think of all the dollar-productive activities that need to be done in your business, and then divide them into two categories: activities where you have control of your time and activities where the client or customer is in control. Then do what I did and delegate the activities where you're not in control. Let someone else handle those tasks so that you control how you spend your time. Doing this will help you make more money for your business.

Anyway, I had decided to hire an agent who would focus on working with buyers. I put the word out about what I was looking for, and my friend Rick Cantore, who has a title company, recommended someone he knew, a woman named Marina. Unfortunately, Marina told me she had two young kids and therefore was interested in working only parttime. Because I wanted to change the entire way I managed my business, I needed someone to work fulltime and be dedicated and totally devoted to the buyer side of the business.

Marina and I agreed that we had different goals, and she said she wanted to continue what she was doing. But before I hung up, I asked her, "Do you know anyone who you think would be good for this job? Is there anyone else at your company who might be a good fit for what I'm looking for?" Marina recommended Janice, who had been working in real estate for about a year; Marina thought she would be great at handling buyers. I called Janice and met with her for an interview. I liked her, and she said she was willing to make a leap of faith and trust that she would be successful working with buyers only. As I said before, she's still with me today, fifteen years later.

What work in your business can you delegate to someone else? Identify all of the possibilities, and then find the right person for the job. Once you start building a high-performing team, you'll be on your way to building a successful business. Hiring great people is a terrific investment in your own success.

As I mentioned in Step 4, I learned very early in my career that the key to success was to keep cold-calling as many people as I possibly could. But I realized after a while that I couldn't do all the cold-calling I wanted to without help. So the year after I hired Greg and Janice, I hired another full-time staff member to do telemarketing, so we could bring in more clients and find more people who were interested in selling their houses. Again,

I wanted to leverage my success in cold-calling, so I ran a newspaper ad for telemarketers that said, *"Smile, dial, and earn a pile."*

Fran Terry answered my ad, and I knew as soon as I met her that she was perfect for what I was looking for: She had the gift of gab, and she loved to be on the phone all day. She started out as a full-time telemarketer, but then her job changed slightly and she spent half her time doing telemarketing and half as our office courier. My business was growing—which was great! But because of that growth, I needed someone to drop off and pick up documents from clients, to drop off lockboxes at properties, and to take pictures of houses we were listing for sale. Fran was great at that, too, and I ultimately hired three full-time couriers to handle those duties as the business grew.

Because Fran had worked out so well doing telemarketing, I decided to hire more telemarketers—again leveraging the successes I'd already experienced. At one point, I had three telemarketers working every night, and they just called, called, and called, using my scripts. When they got a lead, I would follow up on it myself. It was a great system, and I paid them $6 an hour and $10 for each good lead. At that time, using telemarketers in real estate was innovative—somebody had probably used telemarketers before I did, but I didn't know about it, so it was innovative for me. In only a year or so, my business had changed dramatically. Before, I did everything myself; a year later, I had six people working for me. Business was booming because I had leveraged my success by delegating and expanding. If you do the same, I'm confident your business will grow as well.

———

After hiring the employees described above, I decided to add another buyer agent to my team. Janice was doing a great job, but I wanted to grow even more. However, Janice was concerned that if I doubled my staff in this area, she would get only half the leads she had been getting. I reassured her that my goal was to *grow* my business, not just redistribute it. I told her, "I take full responsibility for bringing in leads and for your growth and your production. I'm a rainmaker, and that's what I want to be. So you're just going to have to have faith and let the other buyer agent come on board, and then I'll push that much harder to get twice as many leads."

That promise to her put me under pressure to spend more money, to get more leads, and to do more things to make the phone ring. But I stepped up, and it worked out: The business grew, and there were plenty of leads for both buyer agents to handle.

Since then, I've hired many more buyer agents, and every time I do, the buyer agents I already have come to me with the same concern Janice had fifteen years ago. Each time, I have them talk to Janice, who tells them, "Listen, I was concerned about this fifteen years ago, when Pat hired his second buyer agent, and since then, he has hired twenty more. I don't get concerned anymore, because I know Pat's going to do everything he can to bring in enough leads for all of us, and there has always been plenty of work."

Over the years, I've also learned how to make better hiring decisions. I've had to let some people go, but those employees showed me how to hire better people in the first place. Kay Evans, who co-owns a Keller Williams region in Atlanta, points out in the Keller Williams *Recruit Select* manual that "disciplined selection of people is crucial to being highly profitable."

So, in an effort to hire better people, for the past ten years I've required everybody I hire to work for us for a full day for free. The first interview for every candidate takes an hour; then, we ask the candidates we're interested in to come back for a second interview—which is an eight-hour, daylong interview. Every candidate takes a day off from his or her current job and comes here to work all day. They work with all of the other employees, and we watch what they do. If they spend way too much time taking notes, that's a bad sign: Some notes are good, but they should be able to jot down quickly what information they need. We make sure they pay attention to how to do something the first time, so they don't have to keep asking me or their colleagues, "How do I do that, again?"

At the end of the day, I ask my staff how each candidate performed. And in just a single day, we can tell whether someone is going to fit in and succeed as a member of our team. Making the right hiring decision in the first place benefits everyone down the line. We do this at all levels; it's mandatory for every position. Over the years, at least twenty candidates who we thought would be perfect have been immediately ruled out after the day-long interview.

Any candidate should be able do this type of all-day interview: After all, you're not asking a candidate to *quit* his or her job in order to work for you for a day. Many people who are interviewing for jobs take an entire day off anyway, or at least half a day, so asking them to do a trial day of work should be no problem—and you'll both be happier in the long run (after all, no new hire wants to be fired or let go right after taking a job, and many companies have that option in the first thirty to ninety days). I've talked to too many businesspeople who have said they knew by noon on the first day with a new hire whether they had made a mistake in hiring him or her. Don't let that happen to you: Do a test run first!

———

Some people think it's difficult for real estate agents or other small-business owners to manage a staff, yet they don't think twice about the myriad other businesses—such as most retailers—that manage sizeable staffs every day. For example, I'm friendly with the owner of a local store that sells sports gear, and he once asked me how I'm able to manage such a large team. I was surprised by this question, because I don't think there's any real difference between managing a team of real estate agents and managing a team of on-site salespeople in a retail store. I asked him how many people he employed, and he said he had a staff of about twenty, which was the same size as my team when we had that conversation. I pointed out to him that we were both managing the same-size staff, and although we might have different management challenges because our businesses are different, when you get right down to it, delegating is the same skill no matter *what* business you're in.

Until I pointed that out to him, this store owner didn't see it that way: He saw me as a self-employed *individual*, not as a *business*—and I think he may have had this perception simply because the name of my business is "the Pat Hiban Real Estate Group." The *name* of your business doesn't really matter, however: Hewlett-Packard is obviously a much larger company today than it was when Bill Hewlett and Dave Packard founded it in Dave's garage back in 1939, and the business didn't need to be called "the Electronics Manufacturing Company" or any other generic name for it to become so successful and huge. My point here is that even if you're a solo real estate agent working on building a team, you need to think of yourself as a business, and don't fall into the trap of personalizing your work—even if your personal name becomes the name of your business.

I started delegating—to assistants, telemarketers, and buyer agents—as soon as I started hiring. I was able to hand off a lot of general office work (from returning phone calls to scheduling appointments), cold-calling, and helping buyers find the properties they were interested in.

One job I couldn't bring myself to delegate, though, was my listing appointments: I just felt that if my name was on the "for sale" sign, and if these clients were referred to me, I should be the one to meet with them about selling their home. I worried that if I sent someone else to meet with a potential client and that client decided to list with another agent at another firm, then it would reflect badly on me. I knew I would take it as a personal rejection.

Finally, I thought I was ready to let someone else handle these meetings, so I gave the responsibility to someone I trusted and respected, and who was a terrific agent—in fact, she was my top agent. I trained Charlotte Savoy extensively: For sixty days, she accompanied me on every one of my listing appointments, and I accompanied her during the first two weeks of her own listing appointments.

But after Charlotte started handling the listing appointments solo, I found myself micromanaging her! That proved I hadn't really delegated this job to her at all. About three months after I had given the listing appointments to her, I started crumbling because she had lost a couple of listings in a row. I started asking her a lot of questions about each deal: "How did that one go?" "What commission did you tell them?" "What price did you tell them?" "Let's role-play your scripts." "Do you want me to start coming with you again?"

Of course, after a couple of weeks of my grilling, she

came to me and said, "Pat, for the last two weeks, you've been asking me how I'm handling each deal. You need to have faith that I can do this job and then let me do it, or I'll quit. You're driving me nuts."

So I was forced to make a major decision, and I realized this was *my* problem, not Charlotte's. That's when I figured out why I was unable to delegate this task: The root cause of it was that I believed that *hard work equals self-worth*. By that, I mean that I felt the harder you work, the better you feel—as opposed to the way many people (especially younger people) feel nowadays, which is clearly the opposite. That's why Timothy Ferriss's *The 4-Hour Workweek* is so successful. The author of that book has no problem making $1 million by working only four hours a week, and it's an incredibly popular concept. There's nothing really wrong with that, but the baby boomer generation (and certainly the generation that grew up during the Depression) thinks that if you don't work hard, you're not worth your weight. So I had to get over that, which I did by reevaluating how I defined my own sense of self-worth.

I thought about a guy I knew but didn't respect. He had a poor work ethic (from my point of view). This guy—I'll call him Jack—was about my age, so I thought he should be working just as hard as I was. Instead, Jack typically rolled into the office around 4:00 in the after-noon wearing sandals and really casual clothes, whereas I had been in the office for eight hours already, dressed in my usual tailored suit (or at least a jacket and tie). To me, Jack seemed lazy; I felt that he wasn't giving this job his all. It seemed to me that he could have been selling more houses but simply chose not to. I thought Jack was a loser, and I thought he wasn't living up to his potential.

Then someone suggested to me that I should think of Jack when he was a baby. People love babies *unconditionally* because babies are tiny and vulnerable and incapable of taking care of themselves. It is impossible to attach a condition for love to a baby. But many people tend to stop loving others once they put conditions on them— for example, the way a parent might love a child only if the child does well in school or at a sport. Every parent knows that's not right—that you need to continue to love your child unconditionally, and that you shouldn't treat your child (or anyone) as though they need to do certain things to prove that they're worthy of your love or respect or friendship. But we all know that this is sometimes dif-ficult, because most people tend to want others to live up to some standard they've set.

I felt that way about this guy in my office because I had put *conditions* on Jack—the same conditions I put on myself: that if I didn't work twelve hours a day and handle the listing appointments myself, I wasn't "worthy." So I had to first overcome that feeling and realize that I am a worthy person regardless of how many hours I work or how much of the work I do personally. And then I had to realize that the same should be true of Jack, who I thought was lazy. If he wants to work only a few hours a day and that works for him, so be it. And if I take a day off and don't work at all, I'm still worth the same that I was yesterday. That was a pivotal realization for me, and from that point on, I was able to delegate just about everything and anything, because I had gotten over the hump.

Most people working in real estate aren't comfortable delegating because it's such an independent field. In order to delegate, these professionals need to change their mind-set. One of the reasons real estate agents—and other independent professionals, such as lawyers, doctors, and other solo practitioners—don't delegate as much as they should is because *they take their jobs too personally.* They're simply unwilling to let go of any work at all.

One of my lawyers is like this. Sometimes he gets really backed up with work, and it takes him a month to get back to me, which means I have to keep following up with him. I don't want to pester him, but I need my work done in a timely manner. He will finally get whatever I need done, but I've said to him on more than one occasion, "Look, I don't care if you do this or if a paralegal does it, but I just need someone to look at it and get back to me."

Nevertheless, he thinks he has to do everything himself because it's his law firm. It's his name on the work, and it's his reputation that's at stake. I understand that concern, but I still think his overall practice is damaged in the long run, because of his inability or unwillingness to delegate. He needs to find people he trusts to help him with his workload and then let them do whatever work they can so that he can focus on the higher-level work that only he can do. And in fact, I've stopped doing business with this lawyer because he doesn't get back to me quickly enough. I need someone who can turn around my work on a shorter schedule.

I got the idea of delegating and letting go and not being personally attached to my business from another lawyer—Johnnie Cochran, who was one of OJ Simpson's lawyers in the famous 1995 murder trial. I was watching TV one night several years after the trial, and I saw a commercial on one of the local television stations that said, "Hi, I'm Johnnie Cochran. We've just opened up an office in Washington, DC. If you need a lawyer, call the Cochran Group." And I thought to myself, "Wait a minute. I know he's in LA. Did he move to this area? What's he doing in Washington, DC?"

So I went on the Internet, searched "Johnnie Cochran," and found out he had about seventeen offices, in Atlanta, Philadelphia, New York, and all over the country. Obviously, Cochran himself couldn't actually be working in offices in all of those cities. Though he certainly could have represented clients all across the United States, why would he need seventeen offices? I realized what he was doing was simply lending his name to all these offices, almost like a franchise. I'm sure if I had called the Washington, DC, office, I could have hired a lawyer as aggressive and passionate as Johnnie Cochran, but I wouldn't have gotten Johnnie himself. He probably just cut the ribbon on the grand opening of each office and then never set foot inside again. So I thought, *If he can do this, why can't I?*

That one late-night commercial from someone who wasn't even working in my industry helped me realize that I didn't have to take my own work so personally. I saw that I didn't need to do everything myself. I was running a business, and even though my business bore my name, many, many other businesses are named after the people who founded them, yet the owners know they can't possibly do everything themselves. They learned to delegate!

Johnnie Cochran passed away in 2005, yet his company is still in operation and still advertising under the same name. Because Cochran delegated, built on his success, and expanded his business, it still lives on.

I certainly understand the concerns that many businesspeople have when it comes to this concept: If their name is on the door and the letterhead, any work that gets done in their name may affect their reputation. That's what my lawyer is worried about: He wants things done a certain way, and he doesn't want someone to screw things up that will reflect badly on him.

Here's how you can prevent that from happening. First, as I mentioned, you need to think of your business *as a business*, not as an extension of yourself. Again, my company is the Pat Hiban Real Estate Group, which is a business entity that is not the same as me, Pat Hiban. Second—and I can't emphasize this enough—you need to hire the best people you can find, and then have faith in the people you've hired.

The only time you should get upset over something you've delegated is when you know in your heart that you delegated it to someone who really isn't competent. When that happens to me, I'm not angry at or frustrated with the person who failed at the task; instead, I get annoyed with myself either for hiring the wrong person in the first place or for not letting that person go once I realized he or she was no longer doing a good job. But when one of my agents or anyone else on my team does something wrong—as long as I know that person is typically very good at what he or she does—I'm okay with what has happened because everybody makes mistakes. And the only way to reduce the number of mistakes someone makes is through training, training, training, and more training.

I learned a lot about letting go and not being personally attached from Howard Brinton. Howard founded the company Star Power, which features one hundred top real estate agents from all over the United States and Canada who teach classes on different topics. Howard personally handpicked and interviewed these real estate agents to teach his courses, and they're in the trenches of real estate sales; they're not former real estate agents who are now focused on teaching, and they're not people who are great teachers but have never sold real estate in their lives. These are true business-to-business courses.

People who attend Star Power conferences can choose seminars on fifty different real estate–related topics. For example, they can learn from someone who works in a small market, or from someone who's experienced in selling in a large market, or from someone from a city market, or from someone who does a lot of advertising, or from someone who does no advertising, and so forth. In other words, Howard hired all types of agents to teach different courses, so people who attend his conferences can decide what background best matches their own.

Howard's conferences taught me that working with a team would be more fun than working solo, and he taught me a lot about how to build a great team. Some people disagree with the idea that working in teams is fun— especially businesspeople who have chosen to become sole proprietors or independent agents. But if you want to create a fun or active environment, or if you want to be where there's energy, creating teams is the way to go.

Howard also taught me how best to manage my

team. For example, if something goes wrong, you should always focus on the *system* that failed, never on the *people* involved. What system did you set up, and how did it go wrong? What checks and balances do you have in place? What forms of accountability have you set up? What kind of training did you do? When something goes wrong, it's usually a system error, not a human error. It doesn't help to point fingers and lay blame and yell at your team; instead, figure out where your work process or system failed, and fix it as soon as possible.

The bottom line is that delegating effectively is critical to getting more done. If you delegate to people you trust to do the job you've asked them to do, you can do so much more work that demands your own time and experience. And that's a great way to grow your business!

YOUR 7-FIGURE GAME PLAN

1. **Build your business by being persistent.** Obviously, not everyone you talk to will be interested in doing business with you, but you can always ask them if they know anyone *else* who might be interested. That's what I've always done when I meet someone

who isn't yet ready to buy or sell a house: I simply ask them if they know anyone who is looking to buy or sell—and I've gotten a lot of referrals that way. The same can work for you.

2. **Advertise your success.** Once you break into a new area of your business, leverage that success by advertising it to other potential clients. That's what I have done throughout my career, including when I started working with banks and selling foreclosed properties. Each new sale or success can lead to other similar sales and successes, but only if you promote what you're doing!

3. **Build your business by building your team.** Don't waste your time doing things you can delegate to someone else: Save your precious time for the tasks that truly require your attention and skills and that will actually bring in money. Too many people waste most of their workdays completing paperwork when they should be out prospecting for new business and meeting with clients.

4. **Hire people you can trust to get things done.** If you do, you'll find it easier to delegate. If you don't

trust that your staff or team is capable, reliable, and conscientious, you obviously won't want to delegate anything important to them, and you'll end up doing everything yourself. That clearly isn't the way to grow a business, so hire the right people in the first place. Many people are insecure and worry that they'll hire incompetent people, so it's important to spend time up front finding and hiring great people.

5. **Don't be narrow-minded about whom you can delegate to.** Sometimes the best person for a job is already working for you in some other capacity. Don't let your preconceptions get in the way of filling a position. Sometimes when you give someone a chance in a new position, that person will surprise you. That happened to me with one of my employees: Initially, I didn't think she was right for the position of office manager, but she proved me wrong and worked out great, which really helped me build my business.

6. **Don't be stubborn.** Just because someone you delegated to in the past didn't work out doesn't mean you should never delegate to anyone else. Don't make the mistake my former lawyer made in trying

to do everything himself. Again, if you find the right person for the job, delegating is easy, because you can trust that the work will get done.

7. **Don't burn out.** Keep in mind that if you try to do everything yourself, eventually you won't be able to keep up. Everybody needs help from time to time, so build your business by taking advantage of the team you have!

8. **Find the real source of your delegating problems.** Most of the time when delegation doesn't work out, the problem is more likely the system or procedure you've set up for that task rather than the person you've delegated to. Don't blame your team; find out what really went wrong with the system you set up, and then fix that. In other words, blame the system, not the people. Then fix the system as soon as you can.

STEP 6

INVEST:
PUT YOUR MONEY TO WORK FOR YOU!

"Put not your trust in money,
but put your money in trust."
—Oliver Wendell Holmes

In Step 2, I mentioned the importance of keeping track of your net worth and how much money you are making. This step is about the importance of saving that money, building your income through passive investments, investing wisely, and diversifying the sources of your income so you're not dependent on only one. All these topics are important to your long-term success in real estate.

Saving money is particularly important for real estate agents, but unfortunately, the majority of the real estate agents I know are excellent spenders but terrible savers. I'm sure other self-employed people whose income varies from month to month find themselves in the same predicament that I see in the real estate community. There's no question: It's very difficult to maintain a budget when your income is fluctuating, sometimes wildly!

But that's exactly what you need to do.

Many financial advisors recommend saving 10 percent of everything you make, but I believe in taking that advice even further. The key to financial security and success is to save as much as you possibly can over and above your monthly expenses. If your monthly budget is $3,000, then try to save everything you can over that amount. Even vacations (and weekends away) should be averaged into your monthly budget: There shouldn't be any massive swings from month to month.

Even more important, you should never increase your expenditures based on how much you make in a *good* month; instead, your monthly expense budget should be based on what you make in your typical month—or even in your worst month. If you spend according to that plan, you'll be living within your means and saving much more effectively. Unfortunately, that's not what most people do.

A lot of people will set goals like "When I make *x* amount of money, I'm going to buy a beach house [or a mountain cabin, RV, etc.]." That's all well and good—*if you pay cash for it*. If you pay cash, you're not adding on to your monthly expenditures and thereby decreasing your monthly savings.

I've found that most people make financial mistakes because they make permanent increases to their personal fixed costs when their income increases only temporarily. In contrast, what they should be doing is keeping their fixed costs the same and increasing their savings when their income increases. Once you learn to do this, you can do really well. As you make more and more money every year and put the majority of it into savings—rather than increasing your monthly expenditures—you'll be increasing your assets rather than your debts. But I see too many agents who do the opposite.

For example, suppose a real estate agent's monthly bills add up to $3,000 a month. That's his monthly nut, so he knows he needs to make enough money to *at least* cover that $3,000. But then suppose he has a really good month where he makes quite a bit more money—which is typical for real estate agents, because the spring and summer months are especially strong for selling houses. He might think that just because he made more money in that month, he can increase his monthly nut accordingly.

In other words, if a person who normally makes $3,000 a month makes $4,000 or $6,000 or $10,000 one month, he or she will typically increase their budget—their monthly nut—to match what they made during that good month. The problem with that approach is that increasing the monthly nut isn't a temporary increase; it's a permanent addition to monthly cost. For example, a real estate agent who just had a good month might buy another car, which adds a monthly car payment that likely will last five to seven years. If you buy a second car or a second home or add any other regular monthly payment to your expenses, that obviously means you need to make more money *every* month, not just occasionally.

I have a friend who bought a second home in Naples, Florida, at the height of the market, and it costs her $64,000 a year just to maintain that home—for the condo fees and the taxes and the interest she pays on the loan. When she was making a ton of money, it seemed like a great idea to have a second home in a sunny location. But now that she's not making as much money, she looks back on that purchase decision and realizes that she added a $64,000-a-year liability to her balance sheet. And because real estate isn't selling well in Florida, that's a permanent liability—at least until the market rebounds and she can sell it.

Real estate agents tend to have temporary increases in income, yet they make long-term financial decisions on how to spend that money—and those decisions are *not* temporary. Instead of buying another house or car or anything else that adds to your monthly expenses, it's better to use a short-term influx of cash for a one-time expenditure—like a great vacation or a new TV or anything you can pay for in cash with the money you've just made.

Personally, I have never bought a vacation home, because I'd rather spend money on a fabulous vacation than on a property that becomes more of a liability than an asset. My friend with the $64,000 home in Naples told me she uses that house only three weeks a year. She realizes now that she could have saved her money and *rented* a place for three weeks a year, which would have cost her a lot less than $64,000 a year! She really wasn't thinking about what the property would add to her monthly nut, but once she calculated it, she realized she was adding $5,300 to her monthly liability.

Many of my own financial goals have been based on saving instead of spending—for example, I've set goals to pay off rental properties, to pay off a mortgage on my home, to buy a $25,000 certificate of deposit, and to have $1 million in my investment account (as I described in Step 1). I realize this is contrary to how most people think about money: Most people want to buy as much as they can. However, you *can* set goals and you *can* get excited about goals that have to do with saving or paying down debt, just as easily as you can set goals about buying more things.

I also think that real estate agents and other independent businesspeople should try to keep their monthly expenses as low as possible for as long as possible, because things can change fast. For example, my wife and I lived in our first house until she was eight months pregnant. It wasn't a great neighborhood—in fact, my next-door neighbor was stabbed on Easter Sunday—but we saved a lot of money by staying there as long as we could. We lived in our next house for eleven years, and it was one of the smallest houses in a neighborhood of about two thousand homes. We bought that house because we wanted to keep our monthly payments low, and I knew it was better to own the smallest house in the neighborhood than the biggest house, because the value of the smaller house would appreciate more rapidly surrounded by bigger ones. Making decisions like that is just one of the ways I've been able to achieve financial success and stability. It worked for me, and it can work for you, too!

―――――――

Once you have a significant amount in savings, then you can start investing in passive income vehicles, which pay you money without you having to work. For example, over the years, I've bought fifty or so residential rental properties, most of which I eventually sold, and I used that money to buy commercial properties—like in Monopoly, where you can buy little green houses and then trade them in for red hotels. Those properties account for a nice sum of passive income each month. I still own five of my original fifty houses. These five are completely paid off, and they pay me money every month in rental income without my having to do any active work.

A few years ago, I attended a wealth-building seminar in Chicago, and I met someone who taught me how investing in commercial real estate could increase my net worth and passive income. Tim Rhode is a former real estate investor who sold a lot of property in California right at the peak of the market. Tim sold $10 million worth of real estate that he had paid only $3 million for seven years earlier, and he converted that profit into cash-flowing commercial properties outside of California, including an AutoZone in Tennessee and a shopping center in Texas. All that rental income provides a passive income stream that supports his family. And when the residential real estate values in California dropped by 60 percent, Tim was regarded as a genius by his peers because he got out of California real estate before the market collapsed.

Tim's success taught me how to be more successful financially: He believes the key to increasing your wealth is to set yourself up with what he calls "mailbox money," where you own real estate or other business investments that pay annuities—passive income, in other words. So I invested in a shopping center in Houston, Texas, with Tim, and I now get a $3,750 check every month in rental income from the retail businesses in that shopping center. I never would have thought to make this type of investment if Tim hadn't recommended it. Soon that income began to supplement my other income from the Pat Hiban Real Estate Group. Tim's mailbox money from that property and his others pays *all* of his bills. Tim doesn't have to work anymore, and last year he hit the ski slopes over 125 times while the rest of the world worked.

By following Tim's example, my own mailbox money increased to the point where it pays all *my* bills, too. My five paid-off rental homes, plus the $3,750 a month from the shopping center, plus the $2,500 a month dividend I receive from Mark Schwaiger's payroll company, plus my Keller Williams office profit and agent recruiting profit share, comes to $19,500 a month in passive income. Because my personal monthly bills are only $13,500, that leaves me with almost $6,000 every month that I can save or invest or spend. Moreover, I can also use everything I earn from selling houses for saving and investing. I followed Tim's path step by step, and now I'm doing as well as he is. With help from my mentor Tim and my mentee Mark, I earn enough passive income to pay all my monthly expenses.

Also, if you think only rich people can invest in a shopping center, think again: I got that investing money from what I earned on one of the first rental properties I bought, which was a $180,000 single-family home. I put down $18,000 (10 percent) and rented it out to some college students whose rent paid my mortgage. After a few years, the market improved vastly, and I was able to sell the property for $480,000, meaning that I came away with $300,000. That's what I used as my investment for the shopping center, which now pays me almost $4,000 a month. From that original $18,000 investment, I'm now getting regular passive income.

The main thing Tim taught me was that work is overrated: You can earn decent money—and even a lot of money—just by investing wisely. You don't have to kill yourself by working seventy hours a week, which is what so many people think they need to do. Tim is living proof: He retired at age forty, and now he spends his time hiking, biking, skiing, and fishing. He has an incredible life, and his investments pay all his bills. I encourage you to start saving immediately, and when you have enough saved, begin buying small rentals that you will eventually sell to buy commercial real estate.

One additional piece of advice about passive investing: I believe you should never buy a passive income vehicle based on potential, hoped-for appreciation. A lot of people make that mistake. They say, "I'm going to spend $100,000 on this house because it's going to be worth $150,000 in five years." If that happens, great—you're lucky, and you hit an upswing or got a great deal. But nobody has a crystal ball, and nobody knows whether the market is going to be better or worse next year or five years from now. Don't buy real estate based on appreciation, because when you want to sell that property, it might be worth less than you paid for it—which is what has already happened to many property owners. Instead, you should make passive investments only in property (or anything else) from which you can derive income every month.

David Osborn, Tim Rhode and me in front of our shopping center.

For example, if you buy a house, put 20 percent down on it, and it costs you $1,500 every month in mortgage payments, you need to make sure the rent you charge covers that mortgage, plus repairs, plus property management, plus anything else. The rent you charge should give you a couple of hundred dollars—or at least something over and above your expenses on the property—every month. Otherwise, there's no sense in buying it, because if it's not increasing your cash flow, you're buying a liability. A few years back I invested in a mobile home park. I was a silent investor in the venture. I was convinced that by simply laying out some money and waiting a year or two, my share would double, triple, and maybe quadruple. Today, the $35,000 I put into that mobile home park is worth zero! The lesson I learned from that fiasco was that when it comes to big investments, stick with things I know about and things I can control. By putting money into a venture I knew little about, I had to sit and watch as my hard-earned money went up in smoke.

I also lost twice that much on a loan to a friend. I thought I'd loan some money to a friend in need and make a passive income off the interest. It was a great idea—until he stopped paying after the first year. Now I haven't heard from him for over five years, and unfortunately for me, I didn't get any collateral from him.

In addition to making sound passive investments, make sure that all your other investments are wise. I've seen so many people who have spent their whole lives earning and saving money, only to invest it foolishly and lose everything. I've known people who spent thirty years saving half a million dollars, heard a stock tip from someone they barely knew, and then lost all their money in the investment.

I've seen people close to me lose their life savings in real estate development deals, in stocks, and in restaurants. In all these cases, they thought they could make money but didn't actually know anything about what they were investing in. It always amazes me that someone could spend his or her whole life saving and earning money and then give it to someone who says, "How would you like to own one-third of a restaurant? All you have to do is give me half a million dollars!" For many people, that money was all they had to live on for the rest of their lives, yet they wanted to be restaurant owners and thought they could triple their money.

One of my coaches, Dr. Fred Grosse, said, "In everybody's soul, there is a need to take risks." This is true even of people who are especially conservative and are good savers, not spendthrifts: Part of their soul yearns to take risks as well. Instead of taking risks in extreme sports, adventure vacations, or another activity that's a bit out of their comfort zone—all of which are less expensive than investing one's entire fortune in something unfamiliar—some people simply scratch that itch by making risky investments. And they often lose everything. Don't let that happen to you: Be careful where you invest. You've worked too hard to lose it suddenly.

YOUR 7-FIGURE GAME PLAN

1. **Know what your monthly expenses are—and make sure you're living within your means!** It's great to spend money and treat yourself to the things you and your family want, but don't increase your monthly expenses when your income increases. Instead, buy

something outright—even if it's a new car or a vacation home. Just as quickly as your income increased, it can also decrease.

2. **Make "mailbox money" so you don't have to work so hard.** It's important to focus on your primary source of income, but once you're up and running, you should also look for ways to diversify. This doesn't pertain to diversifying your investments (though you should do that, too!); instead, it means diversifying how you make money in the first place.

3. **Choose carefully what you invest in.** Don't invest everything you've ever earned in one venture just because you think it will pay off big. Maybe it will, but maybe it won't. As all financial advisors and financial prospectuses say, "Past performance is no indication of future return."

CONCLUSION

ONE LIFE, FULLY LIVED:
CELEBRATE—BOTH AT WORK
AND AT HOME

*"Dost thou love life? Then do not squander time,
for that is the stuff life is made of."*
—Benjamin Franklin

Up until this point, I've written primarily about how to achieve professional, financial, and business success. That has been important to me in my career, and if you've read this far, it's probably hugely important to you, too. But when I was in my early thirties, I started to look beyond my professional, financial, and business success and assess my success in a more holistic way. After all, as we've all heard many times, we can't take our money or possessions with us. Nobody ever said on their deathbed that they wished they'd worked harder and made more money. Instead, we all think back on the simpler pleasures we should have enjoyed more of: leisure time with family and friends.

That's not to say that I don't advocate working hard when you're building your career and your reputation, but most people have different goals and priorities at different times in their lives. Once you've achieved some measure of professional and financial success, don't keep working just for the sake of working. Now that I'm secure and successful, I can afford to kick back a little more. So this last chapter offers some advice on how to achieve balance in your life: by not becoming a workaholic, by not pursuing money at the expense of everything else in your life, and by celebrating your successes along the way. In fact, I believe this so wholeheartedly that I got a tattoo on my leg that reads, "One life, fully lived."

———

Around the time that I started really trying to balance my life, I recalled something I had learned at one of Fred

Grosse's seminars. Dr. Grosse started his career as a rabbi, then worked as a psychotherapist and marriage counselor, and then started training salespeople in various industries on how to sell more in less time. I heard him speak at a RE/MAX convention, and the gist of his speech was this: "Sell two times as many homes, and take three times as much time off."

I figured I had nothing to lose by trying his approach. And sure enough, in my first year working with his program, I doubled my income and sliced my work time in half—just by doing what his course suggested. He also recommended focusing time on doing dollar-productive work—in other words, doing whatever will really bring in money, as discussed in Step 4.

Dr. Grosse also offered a mastermind course where he brought together about fifteen people who met three or four times a year. I was in one of these groups for nine years, and during that time I changed drastically in terms of how I viewed my work and life. During this course, I was reminded constantly that "life is primary, and work funds life."

Many people who value balance consistently ask themselves the following question: Am I working to live, or living to work? To have a balanced life, you need

6 STEPS TO 7 FIGURES

to think about every aspect of it; we get only one time around, and you could be tapped on the shoulder by the Grim Reaper at any time. We should work not just for the sake of working but to fund the way we want to live. So, kick ass and make as much money as you can, but then *use* that money to support the fun things you want to do, to create incredible experiences, and to assertively make your life colorful rather than living in boring black and white.

I believe we need to remind ourselves to live sometimes, to do things we enjoy. Each year I have my staff write out a list of what they love to do, and then I have them use this list to come up with rewards for themselves. It is helpful to think about these rewards at several different levels. For example:

- A 10 could be something that makes you feel good—such as reading for fifteen minutes in the sun with an iced cappuccino. A 10 is something nice that you do just for yourself.

- A 25 could be going away for a weekend with your husband, wife, or someone special.

- A 50 could be a week's vacation to someplace a bit more fabulous than a regular weekend destination—the Bahamas or somewhere special (but reasonable) you want to go to.

- A 100 could be a tour of Asia or a one-month African safari, or some other absolutely mind-blowing experience that a lot of people don't get to experience but that you want to do before you die.

At Dr. Grosse's mastermind seminars, we were asked to write a list of what our 10s, 25s, 50s, and 100s would be, and every year, we had to update our lists, cross off goals we had accomplished, and write new goals. Then, we set them as targets, and when we reached certain goals and did certain things right, we gave ourselves a 10. Every time we met a daily goal, we gave ourselves a 10, whatever that was for each of us: The idea is to treat yourself to something special, even if it's only for fifteen minutes. For example, my goal was to do four hours each day of dollar-productive activity, and if I met that goal at the end of the day, I would give myself a 10. Also, as much as possible, you should give your husband or wife a 25—maybe every three months or so.

Here's an example: A few years ago, I did a 50 for my wife and me. It was our fifteenth wedding anniversary, and instead of just going out to dinner, I told Kim, "We're going to go somewhere, and it's going to be a surprise. I'm going to plan the whole thing, and you just need to be ready to come along." What I planned was for us to go to a place called Little Palm Island, which is off the keys in Florida. It's an island with sixteen cabins and thirty-two servants—so there are two servants taking care of each cabin, and they feed you and cater to whatever you need. They bend over backward to make sure you have a great time.

Of course, it cost a fortune: $2,000 a night. But I had heard from a friend of mine who had been there twice that it was an incredible experience of first-class service and a really beautiful, quiet, romantic place to go. I figured that would be a 50, and that it would be worth it to do something extra special for my wife to celebrate our fifteen years of marriage. I didn't want just to do the typical anniversary dinner; I wanted to blow her mind and really overwhelm her with a great experience. And we had a terrific time.

I'm planning to take my sister Jennifer to China with her three daughters and my two daughters; that will be a 100. My family adopted Jennifer from China when she was twelve years old, and she has seven biological sisters with whom she kept in touch for a couple of years after the adoption by sending cassette tapes she'd recorded. But as she assimilated further into my family, she lost touch with her sisters in China. Now that she's an adult, she'd like to see her family again, but she can't afford to go. I offered to take her and all of our girls for a few weeks, and I'm going to pay for the entire trip. We're planning to go when all her daughters finish high school, and we're all looking forward to it.

My point is not simply to tell you about *my* personal celebrations but to encourage you to celebrate events in your life, too. It's crucial never to let work or business get in the way of enjoying life.

In addition to celebrating your own success, it's also important to celebrate the successes of your team and colleagues. Motivating a team and keeping a staff happy is critical to being successful—and although it's a cliché, happy people really *are* more productive and efficient. So I'm constantly coming up with new ideas to motivate my team—from financial incentives (which everybody likes!) to nonmonetary incentives, which I've found work just as well, especially when there's not a lot of extra money to throw around. This section shares a few motivators that my team has suggested—and enjoyed.

I started by offering incentives that were monetary. For example, one year we set a goal that if we closed a certain number of deals within three months, I would take everybody—the entire staff, which was fifteen at that time, plus their husbands and wives—out to Ruth's Chris Steak House for a fabulous dinner.

We met that goal, so I took thirty people to dinner one Saturday night, and our dinner was terrific: We had an entire room to ourselves, the steaks were huge, all the food was delicious, and the wine was great. After eating until we just couldn't eat anymore, we went upstairs to a classy cigar bar and settled down in one of the VIP rooms, where patrons rent humidors to store their own cigars. We enjoyed after-dinner drinks and almost everyone—including some of the women!—smoked $38 cigars.

At the end of the night, when the bill finally came, it was about $10,000—but it was *so* worth it. The team had worked incredibly hard to meet the goal we had all agreed on, and we had a heck of a party to celebrate. That $10,000 was well spent, and people still talk about that party today, seven years later.

Obviously, spending $10,000 on an event may not be in everyone's budget, but everyone reading this can figure out what kind of celebration would be in your budget if you and your team meet whatever goals you're setting for yourselves. Don't go overboard and spend more than you can afford—but don't be cheap, either. Think about what's feasible for your own business and your own bottom line. Then try to do something that's a little bit special and a little bit swanky so that people will work even harder next time, and be happy while they're doing it.

In addition to working to motivate our salespeople, I also set goals for our administrative staff. Once, I returned from a seminar about Ritz-Carlton and its culture of customer service—the hotel chain is credited with coining the phrase "It's my pleasure"—and was inspired by what I heard. I went out and bought 250 $2 bills, and the office manager and I walked around and listened to phone conversations. When someone said, "It's my pleasure," we threw a $2 bill on that person's desk. Our goal, of course, was to ingrain that phrase into their vocabulary, and it worked. To this day, many of them use it daily.

———

When the real estate market was booming, I also rewarded my team with trips to fun places: I sent high-performing employees to Hilton Head, Disneyland, Cancún, and the Poconos. Then, when the real estate market started to soften a few years ago, the prize for meeting our sales target for the year was that we would all go to Atlantic City. Unfortunately, we didn't make our goal. The next year we decided the prize would be a cash gift to everyone, but we didn't make our goal that year either.

Until then, we had been increasing our goals by 10 percent every year, but when the market changed, we could see that we were no longer making our goals, and every month we fell farther and farther behind. After a few months, that became really depressing and demoralizing for the entire staff. I realized I needed to set more realistic objectives and raise them in smaller increments. In terms of morale, I might even have been better off not setting *any* goals, but that wasn't the message I wanted to send either. So I simply set smaller goals.

After two years in a row of defeat, we decided to offer smaller rewards for smaller objectives, but that year was the beginning of the subprime mortgage disaster—a tough year for anyone working in real estate. Even though I'd changed our financial goals to reflect increases in profits rather than just volume, I also realized that I didn't need to motivate my team solely through financial incentives. After all, even if the economy and the real estate market were down, we still needed to keep working—and hopefully enjoy our jobs.

So I started thinking, "What can we do that won't cost us any money? How can we still create fun and excitement without having to spend $25,000, $30,000, or $40,000 to do it?" And we came up with an interesting—and hilarious—series of incentives that didn't cost a dime.

The first year we decided to try nonmonetary incentives, central Maryland was invaded by cicadas. They were everywhere. If you're not familiar with cicadas, they're large insects, about one to two inches long, with extremely long life cycles of thirteen or seventeen years. The type that invaded that year were the "seventeen-year cicadas," which lie dormant for seventeen years underground and appear all at once for five straight weeks before mating and finally dying. During that five-week period, people are forced to keep their windshield wipers on constantly in order to scrub off smashed cicada bodies.

At the beginning of the invasion, I told my team, "If you sell sixty houses next month, I'll eat a live cicada at our Monday morning meeting." Everyone laughed and thought I was kidding at first, but then I told them I'd really do it. They were horrified but also intrigued and impressed. After all, who doesn't want to see the boss do something goofy? And although I didn't really *want* to eat a live bug, I knew from my team's reaction that this would get them psyched up.

As we got closer to the end of the month, they had sold fifty-four houses, and we were going into the last weekend of the month: The thirty-first was a Sunday. Although they had sold a lot of houses that month, I was confident I wasn't going to have to eat a live cicada after all. I remember laughing as I headed out the door for the weekend. *There's no way they're going to sell six houses over a single weekend*, I thought.

However, you should never underestimate the power of a ridiculous motivator: When I came in on Monday, my team actually had sold *eight* houses over the weekend. And three different people had brought in a jar with a live cicada in it. So I ate one. And you can see me doing it on YouTube, at www.youtube.com/pathiban. (By the way, many people have asked me what a cicada tastes like, and although it didn't really have a taste, the wings felt like plastic on my tongue.)

The year after that, I asked the team, "Okay, what are we going to do to beat the live cicada?" They thought about it, and they decided that making me do something awful or making me suffer in some way again was the most fun they could have, since we weren't making enough money to send everyone on an all-expenses-paid vacation. So the team decided that if they met their goal, everyone on the team would get to throw numerous pies in my face.

I'm happy to report that they met their goals that year—even though it meant that the pies would start flying. Again, you can watch me suffer this in "Pat Hiban Gets Pied" on my YouTube channel. I got hit with twenty-seven pies, most in my face, but some on the top of my head, some down my shirt, and one guy even smushed a pie on either side of my head at the same time. At one point, I was covered in so much pie that I actually slipped and fell in the mess. Luckily, we were outside, and my team let me dress in a T-shirt and shorts, so at least I didn't have to ruin a perfectly good suit! But it was a lot of fun for the team. It was obvious that everyone really enjoyed the mess, and the pies were tasty, so it wasn't so bad for me, either.

Of course, the next year we needed to come up with a new idea. Doing the same thing over and over just wouldn't be fun enough, and it wouldn't be much of an incentive. Over the years, I've done some goofy things, but it's all in the name of fun and good business and succeeding at the goals we set.

One time, we set a goal of 101 sales in sixty days. We put a picture of a large Dalmatian on the wall, and for every sale, we added a black dot to it. Another time, we made a racetrack and put a construction-paper car for each agent on the track, and we had them move down the track one sale at a time, until the winner arrived at the finish line.

The goals I set for my team are always above what's normal or typical: If you set goals that are easily achievable, they won't motivate people to work harder and achieve more, right? So when I'm pushing them to sell more houses, I look at what we sold during a normal month the year before, or I average the number of houses we sold during the sixty days in the prior year. Then I add five or maybe even ten a month to that number, or I add 10 percent or 20 percent. You may not be able to do this every year; if the economy as a whole is really suffering, it may not be a good time to raise the bar and increase your targets. But in general, you should always strive to do a little bit more, a little bit better.

One year, I set our highest goal to date: The team would have to finalize 125 transactions in a single month. Finalizing a transaction included either putting a new house on the market, selling one of our listings, or finalizing a sale where we represented the buyer. The team decided that making me eat a live cicada, hitting me with pies in the face, or even making me run all over town to put up 187 open-house signs on the hottest day of the summer (which is another stunt I did one year) were humiliating, but that the actual time that I had to suffer was just too brief for them to enjoy. As Mike Sloan of my team put it, "It's a short window of embarrassment." So they decided that if they met their goal, I'd have to let them shave my head. Being bald is something most men don't really want, and it does take a while for hair to grow back, so for a few weeks at least I would have to explain to everyone who knows me *why* I was suddenly bald.

The team got really pumped up: There were days in the office when they were cheering one another on to meet that goal by chanting, "Bald head! Bald head! Bald head!" One agent said, "We're not talking crew cut here; we're talking shiny," and Charlotte Savoy—the team member to whom I had delegated listing appointments—said she thought I would look like "a skinny Elmer Fudd." I didn't really think they'd meet such an aggressive goal, although I knew they would probably come close.

Of course, they did, and they shaved my head right there in the office. Everybody got a swipe, and they made another mini-movie out of it, which you can see at www.youtube.com/pathiban (it's called "Pat Hiban gets his head shaved!!!! OH SNAP!!!"). Apparently, everyone enjoyed this incentive, because the video already has been viewed thousands of times.

Since the team comes up with these ideas, I know they are good motivators. Everything they made me do was fun; they were ways to build camaraderie and get everybody behind the common goals. And it was all-inclusive: The administrative staff and the receptionist pumped up all the agents so they would meet the goals. As we got to the last days, I heard people saying, "Come on! Two more sales and we get to shave Pat's head!" Plus, these silly stunts worked because of the anticipation: Just like when you're planning a vacation, half the fun is the three months leading up to it, especially the final few days when you're really excited about going.

Also, I'm not afraid to do anything the team suggests. If you have a team, it's important to stay on the same level as them, and one of the ways I do that is by letting them have fun at my expense. That keeps me humble, which is important.

One of the simplest ways you can motivate your staff is by having them show appreciation for one another. Several times during office meetings, I've asked my staff to turn to the person next to them, look them in the eye, and give them assertive appreciation. For instance, someone might say something like, "Erica, I really appreciate your covering for me last Wednesday when I had a dentist's appointment. That really helped me. It really reduced my stress level to come back and not have to worry that my clients weren't taken care of, or that I had a pile of work waiting for me, because I knew you took good care of everything while I was out." Once my people got accustomed to doing this, they did it more often and more freely throughout the day, without my or anyone else's having to prompt them.

This habit may sound touchy-feely, but by asking my team to compliment one another, my purpose was to help us realize how seldom people compliment others and how most people focus instead on what's wrong. We're often far too quick to verbalize our negative feelings in so many everyday situations. For example, nobody really tells waiters and waitresses what an incredible job they do; instead, they only complain when something is bad or they're not pleased with the service.

I'm proud of how well my team learned the importance of complimenting others. They notice one another's work and show their appreciation, and they've even let me know from time to time how they feel about me. And I appreciate that: After all, I need positive motivation, too! Here's an example of an e-mail I once received from our marketing manager, Rosie Silva:

From: Rosie Silva

Sent: Monday, March 05, 2007 9:43 p.m.

To: pat@hiban.com

Subject: Thanks!

Hey Pat:

Just thought I'd send you a quick "thanks" for making my day this morning. You probably didn't even notice it, but that's what I love about you . . . when you said, "His marketing person is almost as good as you." Those words are, believe it or not, encouraging and make me love my work even more! Thank you for always challenging me and giving me the words of encouragement that I need to help inspire my creative side. It's because of you that I've come so far in being able to do what I do and love what I do. Whether I had it in me or not to begin with, thank you for believing in me (way back when) and trusting me with the image of your company . . . which I take with great pride! You are truly an inspiration to the entire team and we may not see eye to eye all the time, but you always make it better. So . . . THANKS! And in the words of the great Pat Hiban . . . YOU ROCK!"

Rosie Silva

I also learned some very valuable lessons about life balance from my wife. What Kim has taught me is so important that I consider her one of my mentors. I met her in college, and we got married six years later. She had a positive influence on me right away. She has a bachelor's degree in psychology and a master's degree in guidance counseling, so she knows a lot about how people think and work. And her personality style is the opposite of mine: She's very nurturing and understanding, whereas I'm very driven and reactionary. I'm an executor, and I can make things happen, but I also need to balance that with the skills and talents that Kim has. She completes me.

Kim taught me to go slower, to not react to things too quickly. For example, when I get an e-mail that irritates me, she reminds me that I might be reading it in a certain way that the sender may not have intended. Years ago, she suggested that I always wait twenty-four hours before I respond to any e-mail that angers me. She advised me not to automatically assume that I knew what the person meant and not to get caught up in the drama until I had taken some time to think about it.

That's an important lesson in business, because you have to know how to manage your emotions and not let them get the better of you. For example, I've had people tell me that they didn't sleep some nights because they were upset about something that had happened with a client. In real estate, things happen that can really eat you up. But you can't let the problems consume you; you can't become obsessed with what went wrong. In fact, I have a motto I try to follow at all times: "Forget it and drive on"—FIDO for short.

That idea really helps me keep things in perspective. I've heard other people who are faced with difficult situations—whether political, work related, or personal—express the same sentiment by shrugging and saying, "What are you going to do?" In most cases, there's really nothing you can do to change the situation. So don't obsess over the past; just learn whatever lesson you can and keep looking forward toward your goals.

―――――

Kim also taught me how to talk to people more constructively, which is critically important to working effectively with others. For example, I always tended—as a lot of people do—to point fingers when somebody did something wrong. I would say something like, "Why did you do that?" or "You shouldn't do that!" But that's not productive, because you're really just yelling at that person, and the person you're talking to isn't going to respond well to being scolded.

Instead, Kim taught me to describe a situation in terms of my point of view—for example, "I feel x when you do y." Suppose you want to tell a client or someone you work with that they're constantly late for meetings, which is a terrible business practice. If you say it like that, your client or colleague will naturally get defensive. But if you say, instead, "I really feel disrespected when you always show up fifteen minutes late," then you're articulating a problem that's about yourself. Kim taught me how to rephrase what's bothering me, and I've found that her approach works much better for everyone: My team works together really well because we respect each other and know how to phrase our problems in a more constructive way.

———

Another important lesson I learned from Kim was how important it is that I be present mentally when I am home. During my first five years of working, I didn't make a clear distinction between my work and my home life. When I came home, I was still in work mode: I took phone calls, and I still thought about work. Kim and I might be watching a half-hour TV show, but I would pay attention to only about ten minutes because I was worrying about some deal or thinking about how I was going to handle some situation at work. I was always in the future or the past, but Kim taught me that I needed to be in the *present*.

The way to do that was to set boundaries and create a dividing line between work and home. I needed to turn off my cell phone, turn off my computer, and get out of work mode. And I still do that to this day: I leave my laptop and cell phone in the car so I don't have the opportunity to check e-mail or take phone calls. I have to do that in order to create a very black-and-white distinction between work and home. If you don't make an effort to separate the two, the lines blur way too easily, and I'm sure this is especially difficult for people who work out of their homes.

I was lucky that Kim taught me that when I'm with somebody, I need to really be with that person. When you're at work, it's great to be 100 percent focused: I give all I've got while I'm on the job. But when you leave work, don't look back at the office. When you're at home, focus on the time you have with your family: Be there 100 percent, even 110 percent. Just like you can change the channel on the TV, you can change the channel in your mind: When you get home, you should be on "family channel" and off of your work channel.

Kim also helped me realize that what your loved ones really want is more of *you*. For the most part, they don't give a crap about the money you make. It's usually *you* who wants more money, not your family. So when people say to me, "Oh, I work so hard for my family, I do all this for my family," ninety-nine times out of one hundred, that's just not true. If such people are workaholics and working fifteen hours a day, they're probably doing so because it makes them feel better to work that hard.

Workaholics *want* to work the way they do. If you want to work that hard, that's fine, but don't say you're doing it for your family when you're really doing it because you want to make more money.

When I missed dinner or came home really late (sometimes as late as 10:00 p.m.), I used to try to justify it to Kim. I would tell her, "I *had* to work late. These clients are going to buy a $400,000 house, which means I'll make a $12,000 commission!" But Kim always replied, "I don't care." She didn't want or need $12,000 more; the amount of money we had at that time was all she needed. She wanted time with me—a relationship. And our kids wanted more time with their dad, not more toys.

I realize there are people who push their spouses to make more money. There are always going to be people who say things like, "I want us to buy a bigger house [or to travel more, or to buy a yacht], so keep working, honey. I don't care if I ever see you." I was lucky that my wife wasn't like that. I'm fortunate that she taught me it didn't make a difference to her whether I sold fifty houses or sixty houses. She wasn't going to feel the impact of the commission on an additional ten houses. All she wanted was more time with me.

I think that's true at almost any income level: If you want a balanced life and want to spend time with your family but also want to make, say, 40 percent more money, you have to ask yourself, "What would my life be like if I did that?" So if one of your goals is to have a balanced life and another goal is to sell forty houses while only working during a certain time frame—say 8:00 to 5:00, five days a week—you can do it. But during that 8:00 to 5:00 time frame, you might have to squeeze eighty hours of work into those fifty hours of real time. It can be done by focusing on dollar-productive activities and by delegating to your team, but you just have to be serious about your goals and stay focused on them.

Now that you've made it to the end of the book, I hope you're ready to start taking these six steps that will lead you to your own seven figures. Real estate is a challenging profession, but it's also a fun and rewarding one—especially if you know how to set goals, track your progress, benefit from mentor relationships, be proactive, capitalize on your successes, and invest wisely. Those six concepts, if understood and abided by, can give you the means to make your job no more than a component of a life full of love, learning, and new experiences.

When I first wrote this book, it was twice as long as it is now. Fortunately, I realized that my fellow real estate agents would be better served by something more concise, and I worked toward something that you could come back to on a regular basis to refocus and pick up some new ideas, especially if you're going through a rough spot with your business.

The mistakes I've made in my career were sometimes painful, sometimes embarrassing, but they were always constructive. The lessons I learned from each one made the reward of getting things right all the better. My sincere hope is that by sharing these experiences with you, I can help you build a first-rate real estate business that allows you to create your own destiny.

I'd love to hear from you if you have stories you'd like to share regarding your journey with the six steps. Please feel free to reach out to me through my website, www.pathiban.com. Good luck on that journey—and don't forget to enjoy every moment of your life in the process!

— YOUR 7-FIGURE GAME PLAN ═══

1. **Recognize that your life is more important than your work.** Try to do something for yourself and your family or close friends every single day.

2. **Reward your employees for a job well done.** If your business is doing really well, you can reward your employees financially—for example, a fabulous dinner, a great party, or a weekend away somewhere special. But even if your business isn't making tons of money, you can still have incentives and rewards, and sometimes the free or low-cost rewards are more fun and more appreciated than the monetary rewards.

3. **Take time to react to a situation; don't be impulsive.** When things go wrong, or when you get a negative message from someone, don't respond to it right away. If you do, you're likely to respond in anger or frustration and just make the situation worse. Instead, take some time to think about it, and respond when you're calmer.

4. **Don't obsess when things go wrong.** "Forget it and drive on" (FIDO) is a great credo to live by: Don't lose sleep over a sale that didn't happen or a deal that didn't come through or something that just went wrong at work. Learn what you can from the mistake, and then just *forget it and drive on.*

5. **Keep your work and the rest of your life in balance.** Don't work all the time, and don't bring your work home with you—literally or mentally. Money really isn't everything: You need to enjoy your family, friends, and home life if you want to be truly successful in *all* aspects of your life.

For downloadable versions of over 50 useful forms, marketing ideas, scripts, employee agreements, agent agreements, and more, visit **www.pathiban.com**.

ACKNOWLEDGMENTS

First and foremost I want to thank the person who helped me take this book through five rewrites, Ruth Mills of Ruth Mills Literary Agency. Ruth, you asked all the right questions and got me to remember stories that were long forgotten. Thank you for your patience and belief in this four-year project. It's a pet peeve of mine that most authors don't recognize their ghostwriters, when we all know that most nonfiction books wouldn't exist without them, so thank you.

Big gratitude goes to my peer partners Tim Rhode and David Osborn, thank you for reading many copies of this book and being brutally honest and very critical—as you usually are—without me even asking. Peer Partners for Life!

A big thank you to my first mentor Erv Norgren for setting me in the right direction from the very beginning. Thank you Howard Brinton for making me a "Star" and introducing me to so many mentors. If it were not for Dr. Fred Grosse, I would not be where I am today. Thank you Dr. Fred for sharing all of your wisdom in such life-changing ways.

This project began as a book about team management, evolved into one about selling more houses, and then actualized into its current format. Through all the evolutions and changes both Jay Papasan and Jonas Koffler of Rellek Publishing Partners were there for the ups and downs. You never refused a call or an email. Every piece of advice you gave me was dead-on. I may not have liked it at the time, but in retrospect I am so grateful for all the advice and suggestions you put into this book. This project would never have made it beyond the first word if not for both of you.

I appreciate the support and encouragement of Gary Keller, whose belief in me has never faltered.

Thank you to my co-workers: Janice Mattson, Mike Sloan, Charlotte Savoy, Erica Carte, Laura Scott, Jason Vondersmith, Joselyn Buonocore, Samina Chowdhury, Anita Mohamed, Shazia Rajan, John Scott, Mike Cline,

ACKNOWLEDGMENTS

Mary Tompkins, Fran Terry, Lisa O'Neil, Rosie Silva, Josh Moulton, Holly Vancourt, Olugbenga Adewunmi, Melissa Volkmann, Lesya Kuzyak, Jason Jannati, Dave Orso, Kathy Cale, Fran Terry, Eric Black, Allison O'Hanlon, Meg O'Hanlon, Jennifer Cruz, Molly Chatkewitz, Scott Kapinos, Rosa Valenziano, Jennifer Scicchitano, Jennifer Poston, Michelle Langan, Priscilla Berry, Brian Duvall, Jeff Tittle, Valarie Fitzgerald, Holly Van Court, Tim and Emily Higgins, Rick Cantore, Adrian Luna, Colleen Horwitz, Jennifer Greenberg, Jennifer Marietta Kain, Jane Benfer, Shelly German, C.J. Bittner, Frank Baker, Joe Deaner, Lois Leahy, Neil Miller, Alex Karaveselis, Leslie Rock, Pam Stevens, Dan Sobus, Emerick Peace, Pat Long, Lisa Parks, Bill Burris, Dave Conord, Dave Therien, Wendy Hess, Debbie Baxter, Jessica Butz, and any and all teammates and coworkers in my past and present.

To Michael Maher, Stefan Swanepoel, Buddy West, Bill Cates, Willie Jolley, Chad Goldwasser, Steve Kantor, Mark Schwaiger, Russell Shaw, Judy Markowitz, Chantel Ray, Thomasina Hood Tatterson, John Fickel, Traci Corn, Heather Jefferson, Tina Rhode, Patrick Stracuzzi, Paul Reutershan, Tim and Julie Harris, Mat Miller, Kevin Small, Rick Muniz, Chris Guldi, Marlene Rogers, Jennifer and Scott Hashisaki, Craig Proctor, Brian Buffini,

Barbara Corcoran, Floyd Wickman, Dianna Kokoszka, Alexis McGee, Ben Kinney, Bob Corcoran: Thank you each for helping in your own special way.

To my Mom and Dad, Art and Ann Hiban: Thank you for enjoying this ride with me.

To my biggest fans, my daughters, Heather and Kayli: Thanks for keeping me humble.

Last but not least, to my beautiful bride, Kim, for staying curious and always believing in me and my endeavors.

ABOUT THE AUTHOR

Pat Hiban has been a successful real estate agent for twenty-five years. He has sold more than one billion dollars worth of residential real estate, one house at a time. Over the course of his career, Pat has increased his sales from ten homes per year to five hundred homes per year—in other words, selling more than one home a day. Pat has negotiated as many as fourteen contracts in a single day.

Pat began his career right out of college and earned only $13,200 during his first year in business. But by working hard and using all the ideas he has compiled in *6 Steps to 7 Figures*, he quickly doubled his annual salary in only his second year in business, then tripled that by year three, eventually earning over five million dollars in a single year.

He also grew his business. Although he started out as an independent, he hired more and more people to build a fifty-four-person team. Pat's current team structure allows him to take off over 150 days per year while still selling hundreds of homes.

Over the course of his career, Pat bought over fifty homes himself, many of which he sold in order to purchase cash-flowing commercial properties.

Pat presents to thousands of people every year at a variety of professional conferences. He has appeared on ABC and Fox News programs as an expert on real estate trends, and he has been profiled or quoted in *Time*, *The Wall Street Journal*, *The Washington Post*, *The Baltimore Sun*, and many real estate industry publications.

He lives in a suburb of Baltimore, Maryland with his wife and two daughters.